D1572361

BLACK SUN OF THE MIWOK

Black Sun of the Miwok

Jack Burrows

EXICO PRESS   Albuquerque

Library of Congress Cataloging-in-Publication Data
Burrows, Jack.
Black sun of the Miwok / Jack Burrows. —1st ed.
p. cm.
ISBN 0-8263-2237-9 (cloth : alk. paper — ISBN 0-8263-2238-7 (pbk. :
alk. paper)
1. Miwok Indians—Social conditions. 2. Miwok Indians—
Biography. I.
Title.
E99.M69 B87 2000
979.4'5004974—dc21
99-
050772

For Helen, my strongest critic who kept the faith,
and for my friend, Russell Fischer, with thanks for his help,
and for all those old Indians herein.

Loooong time ago plenty food for Eenjun. Plenty deer, plenty bear, plenty rabbit, plenty bird. Plenty acorn. Whiteman he come. Kill bear, deer, rabbit, bird. Cut trees. Eenjun he no eat. Beg for whiteman. Bimeby Eenjun he die. No more Eenjun. Sun go black.

Walker, Miwok Headman

Contents

Preface

I imagine that every writer suffers a "let-down" of varying degrees after having "lived" for several years or more with his or her characters or creations. I think it is especially true when the characters are real people and you have actually lived among and with them. Whatever objectivity is at risk, however, through contact with human beings rather than with creations of the imagination, is insignificant when considered alongside the respect and appreciation that comes with a deeper knowledge and personal understanding. But there are dangers, too, those of omission and commission, and regrets. I wish that I might have included the stories:

of Staff Sergeant Ray Jeff, a full-blood Miwok Indian and close friend whose name is honored on the roster of the most decorated soldiers of World War II: three silver stars, the bronze star, the Combat Infantryman's Badge and two Purple hearts. Ray Jeff was killed covering the retreat of his platoon on a ridge near Tsuva on Kwajalein atoll in the Marshall Islands.

Ray is buried—as he wished to be—"under the buckeye" on my grandfather's ranch near Vallecito, California.

of Old Limpy, the Weaver of Murphys, one of the few Miwok women to make beautiful blankets and a notoriously loving and gentle soul.

FIG 1. Walker by Stephens Store-Murphys. Courtesy Lottie Stephens.

of Indian Jim who, after twelve hours of hard labor on a hot summer day, was paid with a jug of cheap red wine. He sought the shade of a wide-spreading oak and drank on through the night. His body was found the next morning.

of Old Yellow Jacket (*so-pi-ye*) who plucked a few nuggets from the miners sluice boxes. They booby-trapped him with powder and blew his eyes out. That a man's eyesight could be equated with a few colors in a box would have been unthinkable, unless he was an Indian. Yellow Jacket, the handiwork of the miners, turned to the whites as a beggar. He carried a *chomuck* (sack) and accepted whatever was dropped into it. He carried a long staff and walked barefoot so he could "see," enduring the strewing of thistles in his path by "fun loving" white children. He rose above his persecutions and inflictions to become a *haiapu* (chief or headman), respected by Indians and white alike.

of Old Lucy whose horribly mutilated legs were swathed in dirty rags. Unable to walk she crawled, a grotesque and pathetic little figure, kicking along through dust or mud by the side of the road or down a ditch. One day (and as recently as 1895) a mile below Murphys, a group of white boys happened on to Lucy crawling towards home. They rocked her to death, they declared, to "put her out of her misery" and so efficiently, she did not even cry out. Lucy was also mute.

I will write all your stories one day, a sacred promise. For now, *sake-ts* (friends) I offer your photos.

Introduction

The northern California Indians were a people surrounded by totemic associations, steeped in animism and dreamlike ritual, anthropomorphically attuned to their land and its animals, held in near classic frieze with all the forces of nature. They might have gone on forever but were brought to ruin by one of the natural elements of their own world—gold. The white men, the Americans especially, who had never learned to live with the land, only to exploit it, came after the yellow stuff, and they came to the foothills, to Calaveras, Amador, and Tuolumne Counties, bringing with them their greed, racial hatreds, their diseases, and their military traditions. They swarmed into little valleys that would soon bear names like Angels Camp, Vallecito, Douglas Flat, Sonora, Columbia, Tuttletown, Coulterville, and Murphys and commenced digging along the willow-sheathed streams. In the next fifty years, according to the census of 1910, war, disease, brutality, and environmental devastation had reduced the Penutian-speaking Miwok population of the three counties to a haunting

670 souls, only half of whom were full-bloods. The 1920s and the early 1930s witnessed the passing of a culture, without seeing it pass.

Growing up in the mining town of Murphys, I well remember those few old Indians left in the late 1930s. They were not "diggers," an appellation gratuitously bestowed by the forty-niners, but Miwok gatherers and grinders, small game hunters whose ancestors had lived "sedentarily" along the interior rivers and among the marvelously fecund oak groves and secluded valleys of northern California. From 1910 to the 1930s, they were no longer simply a conquered and culturally alienated people living on their rancherias and trying hopelessly to retain and observe customs and traditions. They were the pathetic remnant of a centuries-old culture whose existence was now dependent upon the quixotic nature and sufferance of the intruding white man.

There was nothing of the feathered and painted barbaric splendor of the Plains Indians about the Miwok, nothing of the majestic presence of Kiowa or Comanche, Sioux or Cheyenne that obtains even today, little of the dignity of the braided "hat" Indians or the silent mystery of the blanket-swathed Indians of the Southwest. Living symbiotically along the ragged fringes of the white man's society, the Miwok were short, squat, broad-nosed men with thick, spiky hair, and wrinkled, fat, and shapeless women, "squaws" in Anglo terms. They wore the white man's cast-off clothing and shoes, slept in his barns and sheds or in little shacks "outside of town."

The Miwok sang and danced for the crumbs the whites tossed them. But mostly they begged. Each man and woman carried a *chomuck* bag and made the rounds, daily or weekly, depending on the white man's generosity, or on his or her own talent to amuse and willingness to play the clown. They submitted to the Anglo's strange repertory of stereotypes, accommodated to the gruff and harsh speech he inexplicably affected when talking to them and to his presumed familiarity with their language, sat in hostile silence when white men arrogantly walked into their shacks, suffered the interruptions of ritual and ceremonial dancing in their one or two remaining roundhouses, which must have been nothing less than poignant and forcible reminders that the old days were gone forever.

But their final degradation, their utter and complete surrender of identity, it seems to me, is to be found in their names: no exotic names here, no names that recalled great deeds, no names earned, no names expressing harmony with the land, no Sitting Bulls or Red Clouds, no Cochises, no Geronimos. They were given names that suited the white man's whimsy or reflected his cruelty. Dumpy and prune-like "squaws" were improbably called Peggy, Suzy, Tillie, Nancy, Lucy, with Mary, the most popular or common. More often than not the names were prefixed with "Old" or "Indian" as if it were necessary to assign age and race to ensure identity: Old Lucy, Old Mary, Indian Jack, Indian Jess, Indian Jim, Indian Willie. There were always Indians with two first names: Jimmie Joe, Johnnie Jack, Tillie Jeff, Ray Jeff, Daisy Sam. An Indian woman who gimped through town on a cane was called Limpy; two old women, one with a bad tremor, the other with a deformed leg, were Old Palsy and Old Flattire.

FIG 2. Yellow Jacket's sister (no name)— Murphys. Courtesy Lottie Stephens.

Fig 3. Roundhouse and Indian shacks
(burned 1922)—Rocky Hill, Murphys.
Courtesy Bill Harper.

And there were those who bore slave names—especially
the earlier Indians, and those who were very old in the 1920s
and 1930s—names redolent of the antebellum South: Tuna (a
blind man who played the harmonica), John Brown, Johnny
Tecumseh, Aaron (said to have originally been Aaron Burr),
and Walker. A sedate old couple who lived in a one-room
shack outside of Murphys was Abraham and Mary Lincoln. It
is doubtful that these Indians even knew their real names, so
complete and numbing was their submission. From acorn culture and roundhouse ritual, the historical parabola to near
physical extinction—and to complete extinction of the spirit—
covered a mere 75 to 80 years.

By the 1930s, the white preoccupation in Miwok country was with another minority, *Amos 'n' Andy,* who more precisely symbolized subservience and sated the appetite for stereotypy. "Heap Big Chief," gave way to "Brother Andy," and "King-fish," and "ugh" to "sho', sho'," and "check and double check," in the lexicon of racial affections. The faint singing and keen-ing that sometimes drifted in from the hills of evenings were drowned by *The Perfect Song* that blared out over the small towns, announcing both the beginning and the end of the *Amos 'n' Andy Show.* And then they were gone, those old Indi-ans, vanished, leaving only the grinding rocks, the impress of the great round-house and of the circular shacks that stipple the limestoned ridge that rims Murphys, and the scatter of trade beads gathered early in the century from three large burial sites, all of which now lie under sprawling subdivisions. These are the stories of some of the last survivors I knew as a boy in the Murphys area during the 1930s.

ONE

Walker

I have always felt deprived for having only a child's memory of Walker. I regret that he was no longer alive when, as a man, I learned his language and might have talked with him in his mountain aerie and listened to his stories of the days before the white man came to California. I am told he loved the seasons, when the earth changed and renewal began. I wish that I had sat with the *uya-ti* (the old man) before his *kotca* (his house) while he told me of the seasons and what they meant to him and to his people. In the fall, the brown-jacketed acorns, the *wilisa*, lay in raked windrows under the October-gold oaks for the women to gather in the *tcikele* (the burden baskets). In the winter, I would have heard and recorded his stories in the frail, storm-lashed cabin, seated before the stone fireplace where the flames blazed like *hiema* (the sun). In the spring, we would have watched the grass sprout among the winter sere and smelt the flowering chaparral that lay in opulent white swatches along the ridges. We would have listened to the sounds from the *pulaiu* (the valley below) and to the sigh of the *wakalu* (the stream) that flowed through it. From Bald Mountain above us, we would have listened carefully to the song of *oletcu* (the coyote) while Walker told me how *oletcu* spoke to the Indian and one day summoned his spirit. And in the summer, we would have sat late, listening to the land talk, to the singing mice, and watching *eplali* (the rabbit) play and mate in the moon-ripe grass. We would have lived with all senses open.

I did not do any of these things. I have had to seek Walker through the fragmented stories of old-timers who knew him. But I have lived richly with his spirit. Let me tell you:

Walker was born in the Sierra foothills of Calaveras County, probably around 1815. He was a young man when the first white men, the miners, swarmed into the little valleys that would soon bear names like Vallecito, Douglas Flat, and Murphys and commenced digging along the willow-sheathed streams. There is an old-timer story that Walker was both frightened and fascinated by these strange white men; that he thought they were gods from another world; that he hid among the surrounding bluffs for days, watching and listening; and that when he finally approached a party of miners, they were friendly, and one gave him a white straw hat. Walker confirmed part of the story: "Wan *Alleni-k* [white man] he shake hands, he give Walker wan hat. Walker no wear Eenjun clothes no more."

And he didn't. But he had met white men before, in 1844 to be exact. One was John C. Frémont, the other Kit Carson. It was Carson, as we shall see, whom Walker remembered.

No one knows how Walker got his name. Walker seems strangely without derivation or origin. One old-timer thought he might have been named for the scout Joseph Reddeford Walker, who was known to have been in the area and who was especially decent to Indians. An old part-Indian trapper told me the name could have come from the *kalte* (the circular dance performed in the round houses) the *hani* (roundhouse), where Walker's exuberance and endurance were storied.

Walker was not a name, though, that bore any kind of totemic association nor was it earned by an act of bravery in hunting or war. Walker belonged to no warrior society, wore no feathers or war paint, counted no coup, took no scalps, killed and mutilated no enemy, sat in no councils with white men, touched no pen to a treaty. His name appears in no military journals or histories. No famous generals celebrate his bravery in their memoirs.

FIG 4. Walker and *chomuck*-Murphys. Courtesy Lottie Stephens.

Responding peacefully to the invasion of their lands as centuries of culture had taught them to respond, Walker and his people watched in wonder as the white men tore at the willowed stream beds, drove stakes into the ground in mysterious configurations, threw up mountains of dirt, and sank awesomely deep glory holes into the red earth; watched and wondered when the white men would find what they sought and having found it, leave. But the white men kept coming, now a new kind who did not work the streams and the shiny ore veins that ran along the ridges, but who cleared and burnt the oak groves where the Miwok's basic food, the acorns, was gathered in the summer and fall, and laid back the earth in smooth, dark furrows behind the plodding horse and put the land to a mysterious and unnatural seed. The yellow- and sugar-pine groves were cut and sawn into boards. Houses grew from the earth. Rivers and streams were dammed, and wooden flumes carried water to the land. Salmon no longer swam against the tessellated bottoms of deep, clear-running channels. Deer and bear became scarce. The white men invaded sacred places, molested grave sites in the belief the Indians buried gold with their dead.

The symbols of their observed world, which told them who and what they were, were destroyed; the rituals that confirmed them, permanently interrupted. Their vital harmony with the earth, the sky, the birds, and animals was gone; the serenity of a oneness with nature shattered. Their behavior became an explicit reflection of the white man's attitude. There was left only the accommodation of dependence and survival, submission to the white man's arrogant repertoire of stereotypes, his inexplicably harsh and grating changes of voice timbre when talking to them, his rude and direct approaches, assumed familiarity with their language, and his disrespect for their customs. Reduced by disease, hunger, and brutality to a haunting presence, they hung timidly to the fringes of what was now clearly and irrevocably the white man's world, permitted to live in his barns and sheds and chicken coops. Some begged enough discarded wood scraps and boards to build clusters of shacks near sacred burial places. The white man used the Spanish term for these: *rancherías*. The Indians wore an absurd mix of cast-off clothing. The women wore ground-length dresses, always dyed black, whether scavenged burlap or begged or given cloth. The squat, broad-faced men wore discarded coats and trousers, and they pulled tattered hats down over thick, spiky hair with a grim resolve. When they could get them, they knotted red or blue bandannas about their necks. The patience and craft that went into the making of lovely baskets with mysterious geometrical designs and that could hold boiling water and acorn *hartoli* (mush), died in the white man's refuse heaps, which the women now methodically sifted for battered pots and pans and kettles. There was left only the will to survive. Every Indian carried a *chomuck* sack and begged whatever the white man or woman would give. At the end of a day, a *chomuck* might contain a pinch of tobacco, a discarded pipe, a small jar of coffee, a loaf of bread, two or three ears of corn, a bunch of carrots, a can of soup, and several tins of dog or cat food.

Walker accommodated the white man, too. He sang and danced for an occasional dinner and to fill his *chomuck* sack and he begged clothing when he needed it. "Kitty," he would say plaintively to Catherine Gianelli of Douglas Flat, "Walker need shoes." The kindly Mrs. Gianelli would send him to the store with a note, and presently Walker would reappear, smiling, new shoes squeaking.

History's glimpse of Walker is almost entirely anecdotal, even though he shuffled in and out of the white man's vision (but apparently not his consciousness) for over three-quarters of a century. All the old-timers who knew him agreed that Walker liked to talk, especially about the old days before the white man came and about the changes the white man had brought to himself and to his people. No one recorded what he said. History had sat too close to be seen, too ridiculously garbed for recognition. The historical lacunae created by stereotypy (Walker did not look like a Sioux warrior) and indifference leaves us with only the quaint anecdote and vague compliment to mark his existence: "He was a good old Indian." "Quite a character . . . " "A very dependable person." Today's militant Indians, if they knew about Walker, might well consider him to have been an "Uncle Tom Tom," an "Uncle Tomahawk," or an

"Apple." No bumper sticker will ever exhort us to "Remember Walker." We will "Remember Crazy Horse" and "Sitting Bull." We will remember "Geronimo—Freedom Fighter." We will even "Remember Gall."

If it is presumptuous of me to say that I think I know Walker, now, better than those who knew him when he lived, then so

FIG 5. Walker—Vallecito. Courtesy Kathleen Mitchell.

be it. I can barely remember when he came to my aunt's house and sang and danced for his dinner. I was even afraid of him. But simply from what I have been able to piece together from scores of causal reminiscences by old-timers, I have come to believe that Walker, unlike other Indians of his time, accepted the white man as a profound physical and spiritual reality, as much a part of the natural order of things as the Indian, rather than as some intrusive chimerical manifestation that would miraculously disappear if only the proper prayer or ritual could be found. No compelling ceremony or cause drew his attention. He embraced no messianic movement, though he must have heard through the wonders of the Indian grapevine of Wovoka, the Paiute whose Ghost-Dance religion grew like a dust devil over the Nevada desert and sucked even eastern tribes into its vortex.

I believe Walker to have been a genuine American tragedy, not for what he was but for what he might have been. From repeated fragments of his conversations, it is obvious that the old man had a strong sense of continuity, of history, and of his place in it. He knew that the totality of his life was more than simply what had happened to him, more than a personally painful transition from one culture to another. He knew that he was unique because his long life had spanned two distinctly opposite civilizations. He was filled with wonder that this should have happened during his time, and his strong sense of oral tradition demanded that he pass on his knowledge. But there was only the white man to tell it to, and he did not listen.

Walker lived his life as an Indian. He lived with his wife Susanna, at Duck Bar on the Stanislaus River, where he speared salmon and seined trout and whitefish from shallow pools. He sold the fish in Vallecito and Murphys. Walker and Susanna had a daughter, Sara, who married an Englishman, a forty-niner. When Susanna died, Walker left the river and moved into the hill country near Murphys, where he built a small, two-roomed, turf-chimneyed cabin atop an oak- and pine-stippled knoll under the loom of Bald Mountain, a great slumping promontory that jutted northeast from a flat volcanic ridge. The cabin faced east into the rising sun, which crested the shoulder of Bald Mountain. Seventy-five feet from the front door, in an umbrageous cave of live oak and blue-needled Digger pine, a spring welled from the soft earth and trickled into a hole Walker had scooped out and set with flat stones. To the west, the hill plunged sharply into a chaparral- and manzanita-choked gulch, but just under its lip was a wide, flat, stone ledge pocked with mortar holes. Mary, the woman Walker would soon live with, would use the conical basins to pound acorns into meal just as other women had used them before her. In her time, she would make them deeper and smoother.

Walker was environed by the spacious sights and sounds of the Indian world. In the mornings he sang to *hiema* as it rose over Bald Mountain. "Sun need help, too," he told rancher

Fred Kenney. "No sun, no man." He watched the long, looping flights of *palatata* (the red-headed woodpecker) and heard the drumming of his brother, the speckle-breasted, orange-winged *tiwaiu* (the yellowhammer) among the *molla* (the white oak) up under the ridge; saw and listened carefully to squawking *taiti* (the blue jay) who warned of danger and flew in short, suspicious flights, indignant bursts of blue against the green of the pines. And later in the day, with the sun adumbrating the shadowed hollows of Bald Mountain, he followed the vortical circling of *tcuhu* (the buzzard) who ate the dead things and so kept the earth clean. He heard the rhythmic and satisfying "chump chump" as Mary worked her *kawatci* (her pestle) in the mortar holes on the ledge and watched as she carried the mashed *wilisa* (the acorn meal) to the spring where she leached out the tannic acid in the cold water.

He watched the hollow oak that caught the rainwater and kept it cool, where his brothers, the woodpeckers, hooked on little ice-tong claws and braced against ironstiff tails, drank, their red heads rising and falling like wild flowers blowing in the wind.

In the evenings, he sat quietly, watching the delicate *uwuya* (the deer) walking their leg-and-neck coordinated walk in the pine grove to the north or browsing watchfully, long ears working, in the sunstruck grass on the ridges. He heard the *hekeke* (the quail) rustling and chuckling in the live oaks around the spring and now and again calling lagging members into roost: "hekeke, hekeke." At dusk he smiled at the ecstatic mating screams of *eplali* (the jackrabbit). But in the night he listened carefully to the song of *oletcu* who had helped to create the world, and he knew that one day his own spirit would be borne on the coyote's wail.

Walker was not a crabbed and bitter old man living resentfully on an isolated hilltop. He lived with all senses open and receptive, even to the white man. As he grew older and the sights and sounds of the forest were mixed with the presence and noise of the *tookoolooloo* (the automobile) in the valley below, he knew that his was a lingering but passing consonance with the land, and he savored it. When the natural cycle of a day was not disrupted, and he sat and looked and listened and felt, he was restored.

Even on Walker's hill, though, the white man had become the dominant presence. Cattle were pastured among the grassy ridges and fouled his spring. Horsemen from the Adams—later Kenney—ranch in the valley below passed by regularly and stopped to talk to him in their self-consciously gruff voices. In the deer and quail seasons, the natural order and tranquillity of his hill were disturbed by the shooting and by hunters who did not hesitate to pile into his cabin unasked, against sudden rainsqualls. Every week or so, Walker slung his *chomuck* sack over his shoulder and walked to Murphys. He followed a trail down through the pines to *wakalu*, the stream the white men now call Peppermint Creek, where the *lapisaiyu* (the fish) swam in the grapevined and willowed shade of the deeper pools. He passed through the Adams-Kenney ranch and kept to the back fields until he crested Cemetery Hill, the marbled and piney resting place of Murphys' Protestants and indigents. Soon Walker himself would lie buried there and later, Mary.

Under the brow of Cemetery Hill, a hundred yards below where the land flattens and runs with the curve of the hills, was my aunt's home. It was always Walker's first stopping place in Murphys. A trail, once a wagon road, led down the hill to her back door. As Walker picked his way carefully down the hillside, working his cane, he would begin a low, humming chant that grew louder as he approached the house. It was his way of announcing his presence.

I remember the first and only time I was at my aunt's when

Walker came. The resonant humming suddenly and insistently intruded on the babble of voices. My aunt looked out the window. "Walker's coming," she said. We went out onto the porch. The old man came up, using his cane, and still humming.

"Hello *haiapu*," my aunt said. "*Hockinim?*" (Hello, chief. Hungry?)

The humming trailed off to a sigh.

"Hello," he said slowly. "*Hu. Hockinim. Uwu strocco. Strocco.*" (Yes. Hungry. Eat. Tired. Tired.)

He stood leaning on his cane. He was now very old and near death. There was a rheumy opacity to his eyes, and his profile was drawn into a tight, deep V from years without teeth. His high-boned face was lightly rufescent and splayed with deep wrinkles, and there was a livid sore on the side of his nose that did not heal. He wore a white beard, but the hair on his head, clipped short, was iron gray. The front of his dirty and patched trousers bulged against an untended hernia. He lived alone, now, on his hill. When he grew infirm Mary had left him for a squaw-man in Douglas Flat. There was no one to gather acorns and make *hartoli* and acorn bread. He was completely dependent on whites.

My aunt brought him into the house and seated him at the kitchen table. She spread a circle of food before him, and we sat watching. He ate methodically, carefully, silently, with total preoccupation and without self-consciousness, though with a steady and consuming hunger. He finished his meal with a whole loaf of bread soaked with great concentration in his coffee. Then he pushed his chair back and looked at us for the first time. He smiled out of the taut and sunken mouth, and the old rheumy eyes came alive. Suddenly he jumped up and began dancing and singing, stamping his feet: "*Hi-Yu-Ma-Ki-Yu-Ki-Le.*" It was his way of saying thanks, and it was a blessing on the house. He shook hands all around. Then he picked me up and danced with me and gave me his blessing.

Walker always left Murphys the way he came. My aunt would walk out when she heard the chanting to see if his *chomuck* sack had been filled. She always managed to stuff something more into it, and their conversation was always the same:

"You *hockinim, now haiapu?*"

"No *hockinim.*" He would pat the bulging sack. "Plenty food."

"*Minniewooxum?*" (Where you going?)

"*Hisum.*" (Mountains.)

He would walk slowly up the trail, picking his way with the cane, the old back burdened with the heavy *chomuck* sack, the great rupture welling in his trousers, and pass over the pine-tufted, tombstone-spiked hill. "Me hunert-thirteen," he told my aunt on one of his last visits. It was nearly five miles to his cabin.

But there was one singular and enduring night of escape from anecdotal confinement to Walker's miraculous herbal curatives and ministrations, to his quaint remarks that no one seemed to notice as verging on philosophic thought. And on this one night, the old Indian on the hilltop expressed a view that transcended race and culture with a surpassing concept of man in his universe as yet blindly incapable of observing a common humanity. It was at once a sorrowing paean on the passing of his people and their way of life, and the expression of his personal belief that a greater humanity might have evolved in the merging of the two cultures, or at least in the recognition and understanding of each other, had the white man's senses been fully receptive to the external and natural world. Ironically, we are indebted to a young French emigrant, Mike Marshal, for the story. I do not know when Marshal arrived in America or when he came to Murphys. In his old age he was my neighbor, and he told me the story when I was thirteen or fourteen. Here it is, as I remember it:

Marshall was a farmer. In his search for a farmstead, he hit upon the notion of planting the black, volcanic soil on the ridge behind Bald Mountain. He built a small cabin a half mile above Walker's, bought a team, a plow and harrow, and commenced farming. I do not know how long Marshal farmed on Bald Mountain, or even what he planted, but he and Walker became close friends. Of evenings, Marshal would walk down through the pines to Walker's cabin. Often the old Indian made his way up the hillside to the Frenchman's shack. They would sit, smoking, saying little as they looked out across the valley. But on each visit Walker methodically taught Marshal new Indian words, which he insisted that the young Frenchman repeat. He would point to the Sierra. "*Hisum.*" If a quail called

FIG 6. Walker's cabin—Murphys. Photo by
Helen Burrows.

or a coyote howled he would hold up his hand for silence: "*hekeke*," he would say, "*oletcu*." Once when a fire sprang up on Rocky Hill across the valley, Walker pointed to the blaze: "*Wuke*," he said. "*Wuke*." Then he gestured with both hands toward the smoke-filled sky, making circular motions: "*Hakisu-hakisu* (smoke)." When Marshal drove his cart to Murphys, he always brought supplies back for Walker. The old Indian insisted on identifying whatever was fetched in his own tongue: *yoko* (bread); *huku* (meat).

One mid-January evening, a storm came up. Taking a look out the door, Marshal could see the Stanislaus Canyon filling with black clouds. Lightning had begun to crackle, and thunder pounded the canyon walls. The canescent flank of Bald Mountain glistened with rain. Marshal thought of Walker and Mary in the cabin below. The storm looked like a bad one. If it lasted several days, the two might run out of food. He stuffed a bag of beans, a loaf of bread, several cans of soup, and a tin of coffee into a sack. He shrugged into his slicker, pulled on his gum boots, and snapped his rain hat under his chin. He grabbed up the sack and stepped outside.

The rain was heavy, now, and cold, driven by powerful northeast gusts, and water had begun to run in the gulches. As he made his way down the slippery hillside, he saw smoke coming from both the chimney and stovepipe. When he got to the pine grove, he could see a crack of light glowing under the door. The rain poured, and he hurried through the live oaks by the spring and rapped hard on the door, against the howling wind. Inside, Walker called out, "*He!*"

Marshal raised the latch and stooped in, quickly closing the door. Walker sat at a small table near the stove. There was a lantern on the table with the wick turned up full and beside it, an empty Hills Brothers coffee can. Mary had just taken a pan of acorn bread from the oven, and there was a pot of coffee on the stove. Marshal handed her the sack, and she smiled and nodded. Walker motioned him to the table. "Come," he said. His voice was soft.

Marshal hung his coat and hat on a peg. He took a chair across from the old Indian. Walker stared at the lantern. Marshal could not have known the lantern was a careful and numinous method of illumination. Mary sliced the hot acorn bread and set it on the table. she brought two tin cups and poured coffee. Then she padded silently into the back room, her long black skirt brushing the floor.

Walker spoke quietly, as though in harmonic accompaniment with the beating rain and the tearing wind, as though it were a natural time for important talk. "*Timele* [thunder], he talk. *Hena* [wind], he talk. *Nuka* [rain], he come. Plenty *yoko*. Plenty *wuke*. Walker, he talk." He took a slice of acorn bread and ate absently. Marshal sensed the night was important to the old Indian and he sat quietly. After a long silence, Walker began: "Looong time ago, plenty Eenjun, plenty food. Plenty *wilisa*, plenty *yoko*, plenty *huku*. Plenty *eplali*, plenty *unuya* (deer), plenty *kukunu* [salmon]. Make big *wuke, uwu, kalte, muli-ni* [made big fires, ate, danced, and sang]. *Usumati* [grizzly bear] live with Eenjun. Live *here*." He waved his hand around him. "No *anke* [shoot]. *Usumati* plenty big, mean. *Kutca, yatci, no yena-ni* [bow and arrow could not kill him]. Eenjun, *usumati* eat same thing. Plenty for Eenjun, plenty for *usumati*. Eenjun wait, *usumati uwu* [bear ate first].

"*Alleni-k*, he come. Eenjun hear BIG *Alleni-k* come *hisum*, looong, long way, mebbeso *luti, otiko, tolokou, oyisa, kôme* [an important white man was coming from the mountains and from so far away it had taken, one, two, three, or four moons to get here]. He know other kind Eenjun, looong way away [Plains Indian]. Walker, *sake-t* [friend] go Jackson [now in Amador County], see Big *Alleni-k*. He gone. Walker follow, see. Find on other *wakalu* [probably the American River], *tenoka Alleni-k* [with six other white men]. Walker, he shake hands BIG *Alleni-k*. No big." Walker held out his hand. "Little pella, say 'how.' He no make talk. Carry plenty BIG gun. BIG *Allen-k* say name 'Keet Carsohn.' Say Eenjun friend. Kill only bad Eenjun, looong way away."

As the night wore on, Walker lapsed almost entirely into the Penutian tongue. He talked slowly, eyes half-closed and fixed on the lantern. He filled and smoked his pipe. Often he said, "Keet Carsohn." (Marshal did not know who Kit Carson was until many years later.) The rain beat hypnotically against the cabin, and the Frenchman was held by the compelling presence and insistent voice of the old Indian. Now and then Mary came in and poked at the fireplace. Marshal finally dozed. He awakened suddenly when Walker stopped talking. Walker still stared at the lantern, but it was light now in the cabin, and the rain had stopped.

The old Indian spoke again, now in English: "Eenjun, he live with big bear. No can live with white man." He leaned forward and placed a sticklike finger on the turbaned, yellow-robed, quaffing, and ambulatory figure on the Hills Bros. coffee can.

"Mebbeso white man's God," he said. "Mebbeso white man and God in can. No can see Eenjun. Eenjun, he no in can. See. Hear. Feel. White man make own world. Plenty people. Plenty *tookoolooloo*, plenty noise. Cut down tree. Bear, deer, bird, he go. Bimeby white man hide from own world. No good, white man's world. Kill Eenjun. Bimeby kill white man, too."

His voice was free of the elegiac tone. It was as if he were through, as if he had said and done what he could, and having said it, held no hope that his chosen vessel could amplify and intensify his story into an enduring oral tradition. He kept his eyes on the wobbly flame. Presently he said, "*Hiema*, he come."

Marshal got up from the table. He took his hat and coat and stepped outside. He was cyanotically groggy, and he felt as if he had been encapsulated in a pendulum that had swung relentlessly back and forth in time. He knew that he had been charged with a great responsibility, but he was never sure of what it was. Marshal was a warm and kindly man. But an old Indian who probed the raw material of the human spirit in the lantern–lit isolation of a storm–swept cabin was beyond his comprehension. As Marshal climbed the hill, the sun came up, and he heard Walker commence his song. The tree trunks were dark with rain, and the wet earth steamed. Birds filled the trees, flying about and singing and shaking down rain droplets that drifted prismatically in the filtered light. The earth seemed cleansed. And below him, Walker's voice rose to the sun.

One day not long afterwards a squaw-man hurried into the Kenney ranch. He was a superstitious man, and he was badly frightened. Walker, he said, lay dead in his cabin. Knowing the squaw-man's abnormal fear of death, Fred Kenney asked, "Did you feel him? Did you look at him closely?"

"Hell no," the man replied. "I didn't go *near* him! I walked in and seen him. I got the hell out of there. I yelled through the door. He didn't move. He's dead, all right."

Kenney grabbed some bread and milk and drove up to Walker's cabin. He went inside and called. There was no answer. He walked into the back room. Walker lay on his bed. A blanket was drawn up over his face. Kenney gently turned the blanket down. Walker looked up at him and blinked. Kenney looked at the sunken face and the bone-thin body. "Cook you dinner," he said. He went into the other room and built a fire. Soon the milk was warm. He sliced the bread.

"Dinner ready," he said to Walker. "Eat now." The old Indian turned his head and sniffed, wrinkling his nose.

"No eat now," he said. "Mebbeso bimeby." Kenney left the

food and went back to the ranch. He got word to Mary that Walker needed care. That night she and a half-dozen Indians came to the ranch and asked to borrow lanterns. It was raining when they left for Walker's cabin, and Kenney watched the lights bobbing among the trees. They would stay with Walker only a day or so.

Meanwhile, the squaw-man had spread the news of Walker's "death." I am told there was almost audible relief. Somehow Walker's long life had begun to seem unnatural, almost a palpable mockery of other men's mortality. My uncle went up to the cemetery and dug a grave by the trail Walker used when he came to Murphys. When Fred Kenney came to town the next day and told his story, one old man put his fears in perspective: "I knew it," he said. "He ain't gonna die. He's gonna outlive us all."

There are two stories of Walker's real death. One is that he lived more than a year after his reported "death"; the other, only a few weeks. Either way, someone cruelly told him of his "death" and of the grave that had been dug for him. He received the news in anger, at first, then in sorrow. "No good," he is supposed to have muttered. "No good. Walker live fifty year."

One story has it that he went up to his grave and stood looking down and shaking his head. Whether he did or not, it is certain that the thought of an empty grave waiting to receive him depressed the old Indian. It must have seemed to him as if the white man were hurrying him off. Mike Marshal said Walker did not live long after his reported death. Fred Kenney said Walker lived one week.

And he died alone. There were no friends to mourn him, no woman left to keen his passing on the hilltop. Only *oletcu* knew and bore his spirit away on a thin, quavering wail.

A doctor went up to examine the body. "What'd he die of Doc?" and old man asked.

"Malnutrition," the doctor replied.

Walker was buried in the grave my uncle had dug. He ought to have been buried on his hilltop and the hill declared sacred. A cement pauper's block was placed on his grave, and there he was raised to the posthumous eminence of

Capt. Walker.

I am filled with a sense of anger when I visit his grave. One would not even know he was an Indian. I think he should have a special stone and it should read:

WALKER
Native American—Miwok
Age—113
His Life Spanned Two Civilizations and
He was an Understanding Friend to Both
Indian and White

From grizzly bear and a brute order of nature, the historical parabola to the airplane that circled his hill in 1927 covered over a hundred years. Walker's life encompassed it all.

Walker's cabin was torn apart in the late 1960s by antique bottle hunters. Only its impress remains on the hilltop. I used to go up to the site whenever I could to find and feel the spirit of the place. I would clean and drink from the spring, reset the stones if they needed resetting, and scoop the leaves from the mortar basins on the ledge. If it was quiet and I heard a coyote, I was restored.

I went up to the hilltop in the fall of 1978, after a particularly refreshing rain. The oaks were colored and beautiful, but there are houses now, hidden among the trees at the base of Walker's hill, and there are For Sale signs nailed high on the trunks of

FIG 7. Walker's cabin—Murphys. Photo by
Helen Burrows.

pine trees. The spring is now a reedy sump, and a long, rusty
pipe thrust into the earth sucks the water which trickles into a
steel trough. The Digger pines and live oaks are gone. I do not
drink the water. I look up to the ridge and see houses northeast of Bald Mountain. I walk over the hillside and drop down
to the ledge. The rain has washed out the leaves, and the mortar basins are filled with clear water. I brush my hand across the
largest of these, and it wrinkles into Walker's old face. That is as
close as I can get to him. I sit for a long time on the sheltered
ledge, brushing at the water in the basins, watching Walker's
face come and go. But there is no continuity from the mir-
rored depths, the spirit of Walker vanishes with the settling of
the water. I hear only the sounds of construction below me,

and I suddenly notice there are no birds. I walk back to where the cabin stood, and I remember what Walker once told Adeline Squellati, a friend of my mother's: "When you come sometime you no see me, but I be here alla same. I be here if you no see me."

I look down at the creeping houses and up at the gabled skyline. Suddenly a squad of motor cyclists pop over the ridge and come swarming and screaming down the hillside. They cut across the swale by the spring, tearing and wheeling down through the pine grove. I notice in the torn air of their wake, that many of the pines have begun to die. And in the numbing void left by their shattering, inhuman noise, I cannot feel Walker, I cannot see him. I remember only his prophecy, made that stormy night to a bewildered young Frenchman on the spot where I now stand:

White man make own world. Plenty people. Plenty *tookoolooloo*, plenty noise. Bear, deer, bird, he go. Cut down trees. Bimeby white man hide from own world. No good, white man's world. Mebbeso white man and God in can.

TWO

The Brothers

Too little has been written about the North-central California Indians—the so-called "Diggers"—largely, I suspect, because they waged no war against the invading whites after the
fashion of the northern and warlike Modocs. And with few
exceptions—which are entirely notable★—the writings are an-
thropological with social overtones, concentrating on the
rancheria as a tribal unit with its special relationships to other
units, or rancherias, the roundhouse as the religious and cultural center of a unit, the lean-to shacks, the stone grinding
tools, the gathering, and the trading in beads. The Indians as
personalities are generally dismissed as docile, submissive, and
sedentary.

There was no war. The whites were too many, the Indians
too few. But there were individual and collective acts of sav-

★Kroeber, Theodora. *Ishi in Two Worlds: A Biography of the Last Wild Indian in
North America.* Berkeley: University of California Press, 1961.

agery and hostilities on both sides that the anthropologists—
and the historians—in their hot pursuit of origins and broad
outlines of culture either missed or dismissed, in their haste to
categorize and to label. From the coming of the white man
until around 1910 the Indians *did* live in rancherias; and they *did*
dance around roaring bonfires in their great roundhouses, they
did grind acorns and trade in beads. But they also lived uneas-
ily—although dependently because the whites had cut their
acorn groves—and resentfully with their white neighbors.

Take, for example, the Murphys rancheria. Dozens of shacks
with great roundhouses, possibly three, were strung out along
a high limestoned ridge called Rocky Hill (then known as
Indian Hill) overlooking the town. In the 1870s, 1880s and
1890s, the Indian population on Rocky Hill closely equaled
the whites in Murphys. Old residents remember the great fires
in the roundhouses, could hear the singing and the chanting
of the dancers and when someone died, the high, thin keening
of the "squaws." In the 1890s, a young schoolmaster, name of
Spencer, with archeological pretensions, took his students to
the Indian "burying grounds" and dug for beads. When the
Indians discovered what was going on, they sent a delegation
to town and in blunt language told the town leaders that if the
digging did not stop every well in Murphys would be poi-
soned. The digging stopped—at least until the next genera-
tion came along.

In 1892, a delegation of Indians and whites met to discuss
the growing violence at the rancheria and in Murphys. A white
man recently had been found stabbed to death at the base of
Rocky Hill. There had been others. The whites were angry.
The Indians complained bitterly of white men bringing whiskey up to the rancheria and molesting their women. "It was
pretty tense," an old man told me. Quite unintentionally, blind
old Yellow Jacket saved the day. In recent years he had become

known as the Preacher because he took to standing on a limestone outcropping every morning and evening and praying so
loudly he could be heard all over town. He stood up, now, his
staff in one hand, the other raised for silence. Then in rolling,
sonorous tones, in Penutian and
broken English, in words, the
meaning of which he hadn't the
faintest notion, he offered the ul-
timate—and literal—solution:
"Maybeso bimeby washem out
all Eenjun asshole cabolic acid!"
Suddenly there was an explosion
of laughter from Indians who
understood, as well as from
whites, and Yellow Jacket, hurt
and bewildered, went tap tapping
with his cane back up to his rock,
there to pray, no doubt, for the
unappreciative heathens below.

FIG 8. Yellow Jacket with *chomuck* and staff—
Murphys. Courtesy Bill Harper.

Indian justice was quick and,
the white man thought, cruel. Vic
Marshal, just over from France,
was forking hay down to horses
from a barn loft. Suddenly there
were wild screams outside. He
rushed to the window and watched with horror as a hundred
or more Indians surrounded an Indian youth and smashed him
to a bloody mass with rocks. It was a shaky way to begin one's
citizenship.

My grandfather, Will Saunders, owned a ranch five miles
south of Murphys, near Vallecito. Just over a low, oak-stippled
ridge, on the flats next to the ranch, was a large rancheria. The
"burying ground" was on Grandpa's ranch, on a hill and under

a gnarled and flat-spreading buckeye tree, less than a hundred yards above the house. My mother, her three sisters and two brothers were born on the ranch and raised among a hundred or more Indians. Mother watched the squaws fashion the lovely and unbelievably strong baskets—they would hold hot water and acorn mush—from the tule stems and reeds from the pond

FIG 9. Yellow Jacket (note blind eyes) preacher and medicine man—Murphys. Courtesy Bill Harper.

in the pasture. She sat with the squaws while they pounded acorns in the deep mortar rock on the knoll above the house, watched them leach out the tannic acid in the pond and make a thick mush they called *hartole* or *nupa*. And she rode horseback with Indian children.

My grandfather, however unacceptable and paternal it may sound today, was a kind of father surrogate to the Indians. They sought his advice, asked him to settle their disputes, and he kept as many of them as possible working on the ranch. If a cow or horse died, whatever the cause of death—and today, of course, much could be made of that—he summoned the Indians and stoneboated it over to the rancheria. When drunken fighting, which was universal among Indians, broke out in the Indian camp, the more timid Indians fled to the ranch house and spread their blankets on the porch and in the yard. Grandpa fed and looked after them. And the Indians responded to kindness. Beginning with Grandpa's

FIG 10. Old Peggy with my Aunt
Irene. (Mother standing) Peggy saved Irene
from the Saunders' burning house—
Vallecito. Courtesy Lottie Stephens.

mother and father, who owned the ranch before him, the Indians insisted on leaving baskets in exchange for food and clothing or for any act of friendship. When the first house burned in
1889, one of the finest basket collections in California went
with it.

By no means incidental to the burning of the house and
baskets was a singular act of courage by an old squaw called
Peggy. My aunt, a new baby, lay in her crib in the back bedroom. The rest of the family had gone down to the field. Peggy
had crossed the ridge and was coming down toward the house
when she saw the fire and heard the baby crying. She rushed
into the house, snatched up the baby, crib and all, and stumbled
out, singed and smoking, just ahead of the collapsing roof.

Fire had created one fine and enduring moment in the lives of Indian and white which was, by oral tradition, held up endlessly against the squalid and the sordid, against the mindless inhumanity, something the guilt-ridden and sanctimonious could hold to their hearts as proof that deep down between Indian and white there was transcendent love. But over in the rancheria there were at least two Indians who held no love for Grandpa or for the whole Saunders clan: an old squaw named Reed and her half-breed son. And where fire before had served as legend's matrix, now it was the agent of destruction. For the Reed woman set out to burn all the ranch buildings, not to repossess the land, or for any particular grievance that my grandfather knew of, but simply to destroy. With the exception of the second home, she succeeded. She began firing the upper field. But wind turned the fire and several Indians told Grandpa they had seen her running away. Then the barn on the knoll burned less than twenty minutes after Grandpa had forked hay down to the horses. Indians from the rancheria came running and helped drive the horses from the barn.

A week later Grandpa was awakened by the dogs barking furiously and by the smell of smoke. He rushed to the door in time to see burning hay glowing lividly through the cracks in the barn below the house. Then the barn almost literally exploded. Sparks showered onto the dry roofs of the out-buildings and flames streaked through the parched grass. Storerooms and sheds blazed up, then the chicken coop. Cackling hens sailed like flaming balls out windows and spread the fire. The cowbarn went, and with it a newborn calf and a litter of kittens. The mother cat dashed out of the flames, her fur hot and smoking, mewing piteously. Grandpa threw a wet sack over her.

Only the home, now, and the blacksmith shop stood. The blacksmith shop was built astraddle a stream just below the house so that water to cool the irons could be drawn up through the floor by buckets. Here Grandpa kept his equipment: farrier tools, wheels, mowing machine blades, harnesses, saddles, bellows, smithy. And since he made everything he owned—from harnesses and saddles to whole wagons—loss of the blacksmith shop would ruin him. He sat up nights watching through the window. He circled the shop several times each night. He kept the dogs close. But the arsonists got it anyway, burned it the first night he did not make his circle.

Grandpa never rebuilt. He gave up, whipped. From the burning of the blacksmith shop until his death in 1917, he barely made a living raising horses. He let the horses run the ranch, rotating pastures, and when he had to haul feed in winter, he fed them in the open. Not too long after the shop burned, Grandpa ran on to the Reed woman in a back field. She laughed.

"Bill, you almost kill me once."

"How's that?" Grandpa asked.

"Before barn burn on hill, you come. I hide hay. You pitch hay wan, mebbeso, ten mebbeso twenty time. You almost hit me wan, two, t'ree time."

She laughed again.

So there it was, the admission. Another man might have shot her and got by with it. It is to Grandpa's credit that he did not. But I wish I knew what he said to her.

Time, though, and the frontier had a way of settling things, of punishing its own and tying off loose ends. There was a certain tidiness about it. One night Grandpa sat alone on the front porch looking out to the hills, over the charred buildings he had not yet cleared away. Suddenly an Indian ran around the corner of the house. "Bill," he called softly. "Bill." Grandpa knew him at once, a young man called Johnnie who had worked steadily on the ranch. Grandpa was very fond of him. The Indian came into the light.

"I killed Reed boy," Johnnie said.

"When?" asked Grandpa.

"Little while ago. Angels Camp."

"Get out of the light. Get down."

Grandpa hurried into the house and grabbed up blankets and stuffed some grub in a sack. Then he took a canteen to the well and drew a bucket of water.

"Come on," Grandpa whispered. He led the boy up past the burying ground and across the field in a wide circle above the rancheria to the hills. Grandpa stopped on the mound of an abandoned mine tunnel.

"Get in there," Grandpa said. The boy took the blankets, the

FIG 11. Cave, where my grandfather hid Johnny after the killing of the Reed boy—Saunders Ranch. Photo by author.

food sack and canteen and scrambled inside. "I'll be back to-morrow night," Grandpa said. "Don't come out."

On the way back, Grandpa circled closer to the rancheria. Lamps were coming on in the shacks, and he could hear yell-ing. The word had got back. By the time he crossed the ridge, the squaws had set up a howl. Soon it would steady into a keening wail, and it would continue until the body smelled so bad they would have to bury it.

The Sheriff came in the morning.

"Knifing last night, Bill," said the Sheriff. "Reed boy was killed."

"I heard," Grandpa said.

"Young buck you call Johnnie done it."

"I know."

"You know where he's at?"

"Tuolumne. He headed straight out for the river."

After midnight Grandpa went back to the tunnel. He car-ried food and another canteen. No one knows what he and the boy talked about. On the fourth day the Indians buried the Reed boy. They buried him under the buckeye, on Grandpa's ranch, seventy-five feet from the ashes of the barn his mother had burned. Grandpa walked up to the funeral. The air was heavy with the stink of the body. The Indians chanted and scattered beads, and the Reed woman, screeching and yelling, threw herself onto the ground and groveled in the dirt. Flies rose swarming from the body. *Bill, you almost kill me once*, Grandpa thought.

Ten days later, at one o'clock in the morning, grandpa took Johnnie out of the tunnel. Grandpa had been there every night since the killing. Now he had fixed a pack with food for four or five days. There was a fresh canteen of water. In the darkness, aging white rancher and Indian youth shook hands, reaching out instinctively.

"Johnnie, take care of yourself," said Grandpa.

"Bill," the boy said, and he was gone.

I want to think—I do think—that the boy killed to avenge his friend, that he turned to Grandpa in mutual understanding and Grandpa responded.

FIG 12. Limpy, the Weaver of Murphys. Courtesy Lottie Stephens.

Indian violence, though, was almost always directed at other Indians. There were knifings, "stabbings" the white folks called them, and shooting "scrapes." These invariably happened when the Indians were drunk. "Drunken Indians," the white folks would say, smiling tolerantly and shaking their heads. Indians were only killing Indians. The whites gathered to watch the Indians helplessly mourn their dead, to listen to the chanting of the men and the piercing ululations of the squaws. They brought their children along to watch. The Indians were permitted no privacy. They were photographed over their angry objections. They buried their dead and performed centuries-old and sacred rituals before curious and smirking onlookers. The white man's law said the Indians could no longer wrap their dead in blankets and take them to sacred burial places in the hills. They must bury their dead in the white man's cemetery and the bodies must be embalmed. The Indians knew an embalmed body could not go to the Spirit World. But they had to pay the coroner for the embalming and for the casket.

They were now resigned to have done to them whatever circumstances would do.

By the 1920s and 1930s all forms of tribal relationships or
communal life had disappeared. There were no more rancherias.
Isolated families lived in abandoned shacks around the fringes
of the little Mother Lode towns
or in cabins in the hills, wherever white property owners permitted them to "squat." A few
very old men, who were always
called "Chief," shuffled about
with their *chomuck* sacks. They
lived and died alone in abandoned sheds and empty barns.
Their bodies were found after
the rats had got to them. Individual families were exception-
ally large. The white folks
referred to each family as "The
Indian Camp." By a perverse
twist of nature, these families

FIG 13. Indians (no names) Demonstrating
the use of mortar and pestle—Rocky Hill,
Murphys. Courtesy Bill Harper.

produced far more male than female children. In one family near
Murphys there were nine boys
and one girl; in another, six boys and three girls. The boys grew
to young manhood in the 1920s and 1930s. They grew up without women or wives. The few girls married early. Some of
them married "squaw-men" and directed their lives crudely
along the lines of white society. The young men lived in silent
and sullen surrender to their feelings and hopes. They worked
at odd jobs. Gradually, they lost their language. It was of no use
to them. They spoke only English. They drank and fought
among themselves. Often they killed each other. They had come

to a dead end as a people. They knew the cold and empty reaches of a barren universe, and they lived in angry subjection to their feelings of despair.

One particularly vicious fight took place between two brothers. Something of the sort had been expected by both Indian and white. The brothers were the first and third sons in a family of five boys and two girls. One girl married at fifteen. The other died. The five brothers lived with their elderly parents in an old house that crested a hillside swale. A stand of live oaks rimmed the front of the house which could only be partially seen through the trees. Whenever the brothers came to Murphys and got drunk, the first and third brothers fought. It was said they had not spoken to each other in five years. No one knew what had happened between them. When they drank and fought, they were thrown into the Murphys jail. The jail, built by my grandfather and which still stands, is a squat ten by sixteen by eight foot cement structure reinforced with iron wagon axles, iron springs, and horseshoes. A floor to ceiling cement partition divides it into two tiny rooms. There is a steel door in the center of the partition. The brothers were thrust into separate cells. They pounded on the steel door between them and cursed each other in the white man's language until they fell, exhausted. The white folks called them First Brother and Third Brother. They said the brothers were "bad" Indians. No one knew their real names. I was five years old when First Brother and Third Brother had their last fight. Years later, a "half-breed" cousin to the brothers who was innocently involved in the fight, told me the story. In his own way and in his own words, he said the brothers were not just drunken Indians. He said they were not just acting upon intentions they had had all along. It was anger, he said; anger at their meaningless lives, anger in knowing they would never have wives and children, anger in knowing their lives had ended in their youth, and anger even at being Indian. He said the white man would not understand what he meant. He said the brothers were not even mad at each other. He said, "They din't know what else to do but fight." Here is the Cousin's story:

The Cousin worked as a carpenter's helper. He bought an old two-seated Reo touring car with a custom pantasote top from an elderly white man who could no longer drive. The Cousin carried his carpenter's tools on the wooden floor in front of the back seat. On the afternoon of the fight, the Cousin and an Indian friend called Happy were driving slowly through Murphys. The Indian was called Happy because he never smiled, and he never spoke to white people unless it was absolutely necessary. It was said that Happy hated white people. It was said he even hated Indians. Happy lived alone in a cabin in San Domingo Canyon. He lived by trapping and hunting. He rolled freshly taken furs and stuffed them raw into M. J. B. and Hills Bros. coffee cans. The Cousin wrapped and addressed the cans for Happy and mailed them to Rogers' fur house in Colorado. That was the basis of their friendship.

On this day, First Brother and Third Brother had come to town. They could not buy liquor. A white man bought them a twenty-five cent jug of cheap wine and charged them two dollars for it. The brothers walked up the street to the Big Bridge. The Big Bridge marked the center of town. Murphys Creek rushed under its vaulted, cement ceiling. At the bridge, the road forked. Main Street went straight ahead between lines of whitewashed locust trees. Shady Street circled off to the right through rows of elm, maple, and locust. Where the roads forked there was an open space, at the end of which was a circle of locust trees. The brothers sat among the trees and began drinking from their jug. They did not speak. They were silently working up to their fight. It was here that the Cousin and Happy found them. "I din't want them to fight," the Cousin told me. "I got them into the car." Happy got into the back seat. First Brother got in front with the Cousin; Third brother in back with Happy. They drove five miles to Vallecito where they purchased another jug of wine. The Cousin hoped to get the brothers too drunk to fight and then drive them home.

The Cousin drove the Reo slowly out of Vallecito. It was growing dark. Blue shadows appeared across the sere fields. The Cousin noticed the reflection of the moon rising beyond the hills ahead. He turned the Reo into an old winding road that snaked northeast to the Stanislaus River. The road slipped through tunnels of live oak that brushed the Reo's pantasote top and wound in hairpin curves upward to the canyon rim. The river lay below, foamily white and luminous in the moonlight that now washed over the hills and down the canyon; the water poured heavily out of sheer granite walls from the June snowmelt in a deep sighing that lifted on great wind-borne heaves to the canyon rim.

The Cousin put the Reo in second gear and drove slowly down the twisting road to the river. They passed the jug as they rode. When he got to the river, the Cousin drove carefully inside a wide circle of boulders that bulked dark in the moonlight and parked the Reo on a sandy beach near a quiet stretch of water. Smooth water-worn stones jutted from the white sand. The river ran deeply here, and bubbled and plopped in swirling and sucking eddies. The four men got out of the car and sat on the sand. They passed the jug. When they finished the first jug, they started on the second. They sat in a circle. The jug moved around. Third Brother was drinking, his head tilted back, the jug upraised, and gurgling, when First Brother suddenly reached out and smacked the jug with the heel of his hand. Third Brother rolled over backward, spitting blood and cursing. He dropped the jug. It smashed against a rock. He staggered to his feet, still cursing and spraying blood and spitting out pieces of teeth, and stumbled off to the car. He yanked the back-seat door open and fell. Crawling, he reached inside and pulled out a carpenter's saw. He drew himself up by the steel rods that supported the Reo's top and staggered back toward First Brother, who had now lurched unsteadily to his feet, yelling and whooping. Third Brother gripped the saw through its wooden dog-ear handle, holding it raised and back for the swing. The wide-bladed, paper-thin and limber saw quivered and twanged and flashed in the moonlight. Both men were cursing and yelling. Third Brother shuffled forward in the heavy sand, holding the saw up over his right shoulder. Blood ran down his chin. First Brother backed away cursing. Third Brother grunted and swung. The saw flattened against the force of the swing, curved, fluttered and sang, and floated uncontrollably upward, nearly flying out of his hand. He swung again, stumbling, and again the saw flattened, turned sideways and went humming off to the right with such force Third Brother fell.

Happy now ran to the Reo. He yanked the door open and pulled out another saw. He ran back and handed the saw to First Brother. Third Brother had struggled to his feet. Now the two brothers began circling, holding their saws up. They stopped cursing. There was no sound, now, except for their shoes whispering in the dry sand, their heavy breathing and grunting, the sucking and plopping of the river, and the musical throbbing of the limber-bladed saws they waved aloft in drunken feints. Happy and the Cousin stood back. Once the brothers swung together and the saws perversely curved into each other in a sibilant and shattering explosion of sparks. The saws were torn from their hands. The brothers crawled in the sand, found the saws and staggered to their feet. They swung and missed. The uncontrollable saws warbled an incongruously resonant and melodic death song in the bright and warm moonlight.

Suddenly First Brother held his saw above his head with both hands and swung straight down. The saw flattened and braked against the force of the swing, sliced sharply to the right and flew out of First Brother's hands, skittering and hissing across the sand. Third Brother struck out wildly. This time the unstable weapon went true. The fine-toothed, razor-sharp saw ripped into First Brother's left eye, tearing it from its socket, sliced through his nose and caught in the right corner of his mouth, laying his face open down his jaw to the middle of his neck, leaving a lappet of bloody cheek dangling over his chin.

First Brother stood numb and mute with shock. Blood poured from the empty socket and the severed nose and ran out the side of his face. The halved eyeball hung down his left cheek in ropy and filamented strands. Third Brother dropped his saw and stood dumbly in a simian crouch, his arms dangling. First Brother began to scream. The blood pumped from his face. The lappet of cheek swung and fluttered to his screaming. His teeth and jawbone were exposed. His tongue hung out the side of his face.

Third Brother backed away, still crouching, then turned and ran, stumbling and falling and crawled into the back seat of the Reo. First Brother now emitted great gurgling, animal howls of agony that hung in the air over the suck and plop of the river and repeated themselves grotesquely against the canyon walls. "His screamin' was all aroun' us all over us," the Cousin said. "He sounded like he was unner water, it washed over us."

The Cousin and Happy ran to the Reo. The Cousin started the motor and switched on the lights. First Brother stood in the headlights, screaming, the bloody spray from the flapping face tracing the air like rain in the dusty light beams. Happy was yelling.

"Run over 'im. Run over 'im."

"What?"

"RUN OVER 'im for Chrissake."

The Cousin, barely sixteen and nearly paralyzed with horror, put the Reo in gear and started slowly forward.

"Give it the Gas," Happy yelled. "Give it the *goddam* GAS!"

Numb with shock, the Cousin pushed the gas pedal against the floor. The wheels spun, dug sand and found hard earth, and the Reo shot forward. The Cousin saw the flapping and disembodied face rush toward the car and heard it scream bloodily over the hood, heard and felt the heavy thump, then the rise and fall of the right front wheel as it passed over the body. Under the Reo, First Brother still screamed. His screams came up through the floorboards, through the smell of gas and oil, through the labored snarl and heat of the motor, through the gargle of blood. Happy was yelling:

"Back up! BACK UP!"

First Brother kept screaming under the grinding of the car. The Cousin felt the rise and fall of the wheel again. In a daze, with Happy yelling orders and First Brother screaming and bumping under the car, the Cousin drove back and forth until the screaming stopped. Telling me the story, the Cousin shook his head. "It still seems like a dream," he said. "I kin still hear them screams and feel them bumps. They wasn't even mad at each other."

He drove the car out onto the road and started up the grade. The Reo made a ticking sound under the floorboards. Suddenly Happy said, "Stop. The saws." Happy jumped out and ran back and threw the saws into the river. They drove to the canyon rim, the Reo still ticking and pulled off the road into a clump of trees. Third Brother had passed out on the back seat. His mouth and the front of his shirt were crusted with blood. He had vomited sourly. He mumbled in his sleep. The Cousin and Happy sat, sunk in silence, numbed by what had happened and befuddled by the wine they had drunk. Finally, Happy said:

"It was a accident."

"What?"

"Accident. He got runned over."

"Yeah."

"Got mean. When we tried to pull out, fell under the car. Got mean. Got runned over." Happy's voice was thick, wine-slurred.

"Yeah. I wonder what that ticking is?"

"Prob'bly piece 'a brush. It'll drop off."

The silence bore down. The cheap wine and shock worked in them. They gave over to the enormity of the killing and to the torpor of the mournful sighing of the river that floated in rising and falling cadences on troubled air currents up to the canyon rim. They slept. They would not know until the next day, when the Sheriff examined the Reo, that the ticking sound was caused by First Brother's severed fingers and the shredded flesh and cloth and bone of his left forearm which had some-how been thrust into the fly-wheel and had lodged in the housing. And back on the river beach First Brother lay in a nimbus of tree-filtered moonlight, inside a wide outer circle of mortar-pocked rocks, the site of an ancient Miwok fishing camp, his mutilated face bleeding sacramentally into the white sand.

Happy shook the Cousin awake just before sunrise.

"C'mon," he said. "We gotta go."

For just a moment the Cousin thought he had been dream-ing. He felt a wave of relief. Then he heard Third Brother mov-ing and grunting on the back seat and smelt the sour vomit and wine smell. Happy was talking to Third Brother who was now sitting up. His lips, the Cousin said, "looked like two doughnuts stuck together," and were smeared with dried blood. His eyes were hooded and half-closed. He belched.

"It was a accident," Happy was saying. "He got runned over." Third Brother barely nodded and belched.

"Listen," Happy said. "He got mean. Hit you in the mouth. We tried to leave. He jumped in front of the car." Third Brother nodded.

"Yeah."

"Unerstan?" Happy said. "Got mean. Got runned over. Accident." Third Brother leaned forward and spat stringily and painfully into his hand. He fished around with a finger in the bloody glob and pushed out four or five pieces of broken teeth. He held his hand out.

"Yeah," Happy said. "Mean sonofabitch."

Third Brother shook the glob off his hand outside the car. Then with two forefingers he slowly and carefully pushed his lips apart. His front teeth were shattered and jagged fragments. His gums were cut and still bleeding. His shirt was caked with blood and vomit.

"Yeah," Happy said. He turned to the Cousin. "Les' go."

The Cousin started the Reo and drove out onto the road. Third Brother mumbled through his swollen lips:

"Saws?"

"In the river," Happy said without looking back.

The ticking under the floorboard commenced. As they drove, the noise would stop from time to time, then begin again. They drove towards Murphys, dribbling bits and pieces of First Brothers bone, flesh and cloth on the road behind them.

The two brothers of the owner opened the Murphys Corner Store at six that morning. They pushed the green iron doors open and folded them into place with a heavy clanging. They lowered the striped awning from the tin roof and hosed down the crescent of cement that fronted the store and narrowed into sidewalks on either side. Little pools of water lay in worn concavities. The brothers stood on the cool cement smoking when the Reo came ticking around the corner.

"Something wrong with that Reo." one of them said.

"Yeah. Something wrong with them Injuns, too. Look scared. Sure as hell been up to something."

The brothers were middle-aged, tough and cynical. One, a cattleman, had been a wild young cowboy who had served a stint in prison for rustling, a subject, I was warned as child, never to be mentioned. Murphys closed protectively around its own. The other brother, the older one, had been a blacksmith and a hard-rock miner. He had gone to Alaska on the Gold Rush and made his "pile." "He's rich," one man said. "Must be worth four, five thousand dollars." The brothers had given over their interest in the Corner Store to their older sister in exchange for board when they were around. Now as they watched and heard the Reo ticking up the road, they saw the dribble in its wake. They walked into the road. Chunks of flesh lay strewn about, some of it bloodily ground up and stippled with shreds of blue shirt denim. The younger brother bent and picked something up.

"Look," he said. He held two fingers that had been jaggedly ripped from a hand, but incongruously, the nails were clear and untouched.

"Better call old Whoopie Ki-Yo," his brother said. "I'll get a shovel and scrape some of this stuff up. There's a dead Injun out there somewhere." The younger brother carried the severed fingers to a wooden bench and set them down with the nails up. Then he went into the store and cranked up the phone. Old Whoopee Ki-Yo was the county sheriff.

The Sheriff had come to our county from another jurisdiction where he had been a deputy. It was said that his father

had been a U.S. Marshal and friend of Wyatt Earp and Bat
Masterson, his grandfather a Texas sheriff who had arrested
the outlaw, Bill Longley. Thus he sprouted from promising
soil. He had been a deputy in our county for a little over six
months when the sheriff announced that he would not stand
for re-election. The new deputy promptly declared his candi-
dacy. He won easily over two other deputies, both local men
of considerable experience. Most folks admitted to voting for
the Sheriff because he "looked like a sheriff." Six feet seven
inches tall—two inches taller in his high heeled, Coffeeville
half-boots—broad-shouldered and expressionless of face and
eye. The Sheriff looked down on other mortals with Olym-
pian insouciance. His hair was dark and wiry, shot with gray.
His age, though doubtless a matter of record, was never pub-
lished. He appeared suspended somewhere between late youth
and early middle-age. He was unmarried. He spoke only when
it was necessary. He was calm, stoical. He rarely smiled. He
seemed the Strong, Silent Man of the West. It was said he had
seen too many Gary Cooper movies. He wore a Gary Cooper
type Stetson. He even said "yup."*

Now the Sheriff and a deputy drove up to the Corner Store.
The car had no top so the Sheriff could sit tall. The Sheriff did
not get out of the car: he dismounted. He swung his long legs
over the door and stepped down, one foot at a time. With his
great height, he was a formidable figure, despite some incipi-
ent middle-age spread. He walked over to the brothers.

"Howdy," he said.

The brothers nodded.

"You got a dead Injun here?" he asked.

"No," the older brother said. "We ain't got no dead Injun.
There's one around somewhere."

---

* The Sheriff had met Gary Cooper when the actor made the movie *Fighting Caravans* at the Calaveras Big Trees state park.

"How you know he's dead?"

"Well if he ain't," older brother said, "he's probably wishing to hell he was." He pointed to the pile of flesh and bone and blue shirt he had gathered. Younger brother brought over the severed fingers.

"How you know its an Injun?"

"Well," older brother said, "why not go up and ask 'em? All this stuff fell off their car."

"Them the ones live up yonder, on the hill?"

"Them's the ones."

"How many?"

"Three. One they call Third Brother, his cousin, a kid, and a mean little bastard they call Happy."

The Sheriff touched the brim of his Gary Cooper hat. "Obliged," he said, and drove off.

A half mile from the Corner Store, the Sheriff turned left into a barnyard. A dirt road squeezed between two large barns and opened onto a lane, on either side of which ran six strand, tautly strung barbed-wire stapled to yellow cedar posts. On the left was an apple orchard, whimsically planted by its eccentric owner to represent the random growth of a natural forest, and in the middle of which stood a sagging, latticed arbor. The owner permitted picnics in her apple forest so long as it was left clean. On the right, a round hill rose sharply, beginning the undulating swell of foothills that became mountains which rolled upward, finally, to the paleocrystic peaks of the Sierra. Midway up the hill was the "Indian Camp," a ramshackle eighteen-seventies house breasting a shallow swale rimmed in front by full-growth live oaks. A deeply rutted road turned off the lane and rose in a gradual circle to the house. The barbed wire gate was open and lay crumpled on the ground. The Reo's pantasote top rose above the crest of the swale. Third Brother and the Cousin stood watching as the Sheriff drove through the gate, geared down, and began the crawl up the hill.

The Sheriff drove his car onto the flat and dismounted. He walked slowly up to Third Brother and the Cousin. The deputy went over to look at the Reo. Two old Indians, the father and mother, stood back under the oaks. The woman wore a long black skirt and gray blouse. The Sheriff could see other people moving about inside the house. He touched his Gary Cooper hat.

"Howdy," he said. "You have some trouble up here?"

Third Brother laughed nervously, nodded, and shrugged. "Yuh," he said.

"Somebody get hurt, killed?"

"Yuh."

"Killed?"

"Yuh." The slight, nervous laugh and shrug.

"Who?"

Again the quick, nervous laugh.

"Brother."

"How?"

"HE got runned over."

Third Brother always emphasized the first word especially if it were he, I, it, you, she, or we.

"Where?"

"Stanislaus River."

"What happened to your mouth?"

"HE hit me."

"So you ran over him?"

"WE tried to go. HE got in front of car. Got runned over."

The deputy came up. His face was white. "Jesus Christ," he said, "the bottom of the car's covered with blood and clumps of meat."

The Sheriff turned to the Cousin. "What's your story?"

The boy remembered what Happy had said. "It was a accident," he said. "He got runned over. Got mean. We tried to pull out, he fell unner the car. Got runned over. Accident."

"Who was driving?"

"I was," the Cousin said.

The Sheriff turned to Third Brother. "Where's the other one," he asked, "one they call Happy?"

Third Brother jerked his head toward his shoulder. "HE left."

"Left for where?"

"Sanamingo."

"Where the hell's that?"

"San Domingo," the deputy said. "San Domingo's a crick."

"What's he doing there?" The Sheriff asked.

"HE lives there."

"He has a house?"

"Cabin."

"All right," the Sheriff said. "We'll get him tomorrow. Let's go down to the Stanislaus River and see what the hell happened."

The deputy searched Third Brother. He had a knife, but there were no bloodstains on it. The Cousin had no knife. The Sheriff put the handcuffs on Third Brother. He did not cuff the Cousin. He motioned them into the back seat of his car. Then he went over and looked under the Reo. He stood up quickly. He shook his head. He nodded to the deputy.

"Christ!"

And now the mother and father came forward. There was no anger in their faces, only sadness and defeat and resignation. Anger would have been a luxury. Doubtless the irony of their lives had not occurred to them, engulfed as it must have been in the deeps of their sorrows. Their problems, their degradation had been created by the white man who now presided righteously over his creation, in this instance in the form of a sheriff engrossed in infantile role-playing while tending a real tragedy, and whose very size was both a symbolic and naked

reproach. The old woman leaned forward and spoke softly to Third Brother in the Penutian tongue. Her flat-browed face was webbed with deep wrinkles. Her hair was nearly white. Her name was Annie Joe. I remember her well. She had a beautiful smile, and when I visited her two younger sons, she smiled and called me Chackie and gave me acorn bread, sweetened with wild blackberries.

From the back seat of the Sheriff's car, Third Brother responded tersely to his mother. She began to cry quietly, moving her head slightly from side to side. Her man stepped forward and put his hand on her shoulder.

"C'mon," the Sheriff said, "Let's go."

All this the Cousin told me years later. It was understood that one day I would write it all down. "There won't be any Indians before long," he had said. "All I'm tellin' you might never have happened. Nobody cares. We're just *Injuns*. Maybe we were never here, never lived. If you write it, it happened. We were here, we lived." He had a sense of history. And he told me about going to the river with the Sheriff:

The Sheriff stopped at the Corner Store. He asked to use the phone. He called the Coroner at Angels Camp whom he asked to meet him in Vallecito. Outside, a small group had gathered around the Sheriff's car. They were talking to Third Brother who shrugged, laughed his quick, nervous laugh and answered no questions. He simply said First Brother was dead, got runned over, accident. The Cousin did not talk. The Sheriff came over to the car. "All right," he said, "too much palaver." He had heard Gary Cooper use the expression in a movie. He was picking up the lingo. He put his left foot on the running board and swung into the seat. If you were the driver, you mounted up on the same side you mounted a horse. He touched his Gary Cooper hat and drove off.

The Coroner was waiting in Vallecito. He drove a long, black hearse with dark-glassed and curtained windows. The Coroner was a tiny, elderly man, bald with a fringe of white hair, a tiny, beaked nose, and unusually red lips, which he licked nervously. He never smiled, as though each death he attended was a personal sorrow. Some folks pretended to suspect him of necrophilia. They made jokes of clandestine meetings with female corpses in his morgue in the dead of night. It was said he carried a small, lead club against the possibility of a corpse showing signs of life. The Coroner was philosophic. He knew that macabre jokes followed his profession. Actually, he was a kindly old man who always used the word "remains," never "body." He rolled the r's on "rremains." He considered "body" a poignant reminder to the survivors of the mortal being, while "rremains" offered both transition and finality. He did not haul bodies to graveyards, he "conveyed" them. His funerary concerns were thoughtful and personal. Now he drove his hearse behind the Sheriff's car down the narrow and winding road to the Stanislaus River. The Sheriff turned in where Third Brother directed him.

First Brother lay inside the circle of mortar-pocked rocks. Flies swarmed over his mutilated face. His bowels had moved after death and streams of coprophagous beetles poured through rips in his lower pants. His left hand was a mangled stump. The deputy became sick. The Sheriff turned away. The little bald Coroner examined the body. He brushed away the flies and saw the dangling eyeball, the halved nose and the flapjack-size lappet of cheek and neck that flopped into the sand, showing the bared teeth. By his count, the body bore impress of a dozen or more wheel tracks. He went over to the Sheriff and the deputy, both of whom had tied bandannas around their faces and over their noses.

"Sheriff," he said, "its not a pretty sight, but you need to look." They walked over to the body.

"Jesus!" The Sheriff said, his voice muted inside the bandanna. "Wheel tracks all around him."

"Yes," the Coroner said. "He was run over at least a dozen times. But the face—look at the face."

"Jesus," the Sheriff said again.

"Yes," the Coroner said, "it's a horrible wound, but it was not made by the car. There's not a speck of grease on it or in it. There would have been grease, if he had been ripped by the car. Terrible as it is, it's a clean wound."

"Knife?" the Sheriff asked, turning from the sight. "No," the Coroner said. "A large weapon of some sort. It cut into the hard bone above the eye, the skull bone, and it cut clean through the nose bone. It had to be swung, like a saber."

The Sheriff walked over to his car. Third Brother and the Cousin remained in the back seat.

"You three fuckers killed 'im." he said.

The Indians said nothing.

"Well, didn't yuh? That why the one you call Happy ran?"

Third Brother said, "HE got runned over."

"Well he sure as hell did," the Sheriff said. "Over and over and over."

Third Brother laughed his nervous laugh.

The Sheriff towered over the car. He leaned over. "What'd you use to cut his face like that?"

"HE got runned over. Accident."

"Oh shit," the Sheriff said. "Runned over. Runned over, my ass!"

Again, the nervous laugh.

The deputy stood by the edge of the river. He had been sick. The Coroner was talking to him. The Sheriff walked up. "Those bastards won't admit anything." he said. "Just keep saying, 'He got runned over.'" The deputy said he had searched the inside of the Reo. There was a tool box, but no weapon, nothing with blood on it. The Coroner said they might have thrown it from the higher road, into the canyon. They shuffled about, kicking at the sand. They looked in the brush. They stood by the river talking.

"I couldn't believe it," the Cousin told me. "They stood right there, lookin' at the river and never thought somethin' could be throwed in it."

The Coroner rolled First Brother onto a canvas tarp and rolled him up. The Sheriff and the deputy helped put him in the hearse. The Coroner took the body to his mortuary in Angels Camp. The Sheriff took Third Brother to Sonora in Tuolumne County and lodged him in jail. Sonora was out of the Sheriff's jurisdiction, but their jail facilities were more adequate than those in Calaveras County. He brought the Cousin to Murphys and told him not to leave his father's home until further notice.

The next day The Last Horseback Sheriff, as the Sheriff was fond of calling himself (this in celebration of two or three spavined and dispirited old nags he kept against the possible need to pursue outlaws beyond the purlieus of habitation and auto transport), and two deputies went into San Domingo Canyon to arrest Happy. Whatever the Sheriff's pretensions, the attempt to bag Happy was not destined to be inscribed upon the annals of western lore alongside the O.K. Corral. The Sheriff seems to have made no inquiries as to Happy's character, of what might be expected of a notoriously angry man who had fled guiltily from almost certain charges of murder to what was doubtless a hideout cabin. Happy's cabin hugged the base of a high, rocky ridge from which jutted a narrow promontory, or neck, reaching to the banks of San Domingo Creek. The ridges here roll northeast in sharp, undulating waves, between which run deep rocky and narrow passages. Green spreading buckeye trees bloom like huge flowers from cracks in the gray-blue rocks. Happy's shack lay leeward of one of these passes but with immediate access to it.

The Sheriff and his deputies left their car at the mouth of the canyon. San Domingo Creek is a tumble of boulders laved by graceful water falls, and farther up, alder-draped pools run deep and clear. The three men worked their way through thick willow growth and over rocks. Unbelievably, when they came to the promontory, one of the deputies said later, they walked right up the slope and stood on the flat directly before Happy's cabin. The cabin appeared deserted. The Sheriff holstered his revolver, cupped his hands, and in his deep, stentorian voice shouted "COME OUT WITH YOUR HANDS UP!"

The Sheriff's hands were still cupped to his mouth when his answer came in a shattering and continuous burst of gunfire almost in their faces. Bullets kicked up spouts of turf in front of them and whined off rocks. The reports slammed deafeningly back and forth against the canyon walls. Lashed by terror, the three men literally dived over the lip of the promontory and rolled and ran to the equivocal safety of the willows and rocks while bullets slashed through the foliage and sang off boulders. History cannot see the flight of the Sheriff and his deputies down the brushy and bouldered canyon when the shooting ceased, but the scratches, cuts, bruises, and torn clothing bore eloquent testimony of its headlong nature.

That evening the badly shaken Sheriff and his two deputies presided over a citizens' council of war. They had walked into a full-scale Indian ambush, he said. He estimated there were four or five men hidden among the boulders around and above the cabin. The shooting seemed to come from everywhere. He swore in ten deputies, several of whom were old-timers, the sort not easily spooked. They would leave for the cabin at day-light. The Sheriff was committed to the flood.

The next morning shortly after daylight, three carloads of

heavily-armed possemen arrived at the mouth of San Domingo Creek and began laboriously picking their way up the canyon. An hour or better later, they arrived at the base of the promontory on which stood Happy's cabin. The Sheriff, now firmly in command, his star glittering on his black Gary Cooper vest, deployed his deputies to his left and right and gave the signal to move forward. On the rim of the promontory, he raised his hand. Halted, the posse formed a half-circle before the cabin. One posseman thought the tiny shack looked pitiful. But this was the Sheriff's moment. Glory would be his this day. Under the panoply of a dozen guns, he strode forward and hailed the cabin. "COME OUT WITH YOUR HANDS UP!" When there was no response, he boldly advanced and kicked the door open. On the cabin wall directly opposite the open door and in foot-high letters still wet with black tar that Happy used for caulking wall cracks was scrawled:

FUCK U

Happy could not write the addresses of companies to which he shipped furs; but he had mastered the more earthy, and in this instance germane, expressions of the written language.

The deputies fanned out among the boulders above the cabin. Within minutes one of the older men called out, "up here." In a tight scatter on the ground behind two boulders with a shoulder-high space between them, were eight or nine .30–30 shell casings.

"Only one Injun," the deputy said dryly, "only one set of tracks. Never shot to kill. Couldn't of missed at this range."

Happy had paused long enough to print his welcome on the wall of his shack, then slipped through the narrow, boulder-strewn pass and on into Indian myth and legend as a sometimes vengeful specter who roamed the vast reaches of the high Sierra peaks. He was never seen again in the flesh.

We are not privy to the mood or conversations of the posse as it struggled through brush and over boulders on its return to the cars. Certainly there must have been disgust, even anger. Word of the fiasco was bound to leak out, and of course, it did. A little screed clandestinely printed over in Angels Camp celebrated the event with malicious glee in a squib titled *Indian Wins War.* Comparing the event to the Custer fight, the author allowed that Custer had at least stayed and fought while the Sheriff narrowly escaped death by breaking his neck in head-long flight. The next day, the Sheriff "bravely" returned with "a small army" only to find Happy's earthy sentiments (obviously shared by the author of the piece) expressed on his cabin wall. With some pretensions to the classics, the author concluded the squib with a rather appropriate nursery rhyme:

> The King with twice ten-thousand men
> Marched up the hill and then
> The King with twice ten-thousand men
> Marched back down again.

Three days after First Brother's death, the family made a "cry" ceremony for him. It lasted four days. The ceremony was both an expiation and a purging of grief. It was made on the swale behind the rim of live oaks around and behind their house. Indians began arriving in the morning. They came up the lane in old cars. Many came on foot, a few rode old and skinny horses whose parchment hides were corrugated with protruding ribs. The older women wore gray, long-sleeved blouses and ankle-length black skirts. Some of the younger women wore colored blouses. The men were garbed in a mix of castoff clothing. They all wore hats and knotted bandannas, blue or red, about their necks. They did not look at the white people who had gathered in the orchard to watch. Each new arrival was greeted with the piercing ululations of shared grief.

In the afternoon, my uncle had come by and asked if my mother, my two older sisters, and I would like to go up to the orchard and "watch the Injuns ki-yi." My mother did not want to go. She had been raised among Indians. Their privacy and grief ought to be respected, she said. She relented, finally, to our begging. The orchard was filled with townsfolk who had brought lunches. White tablecloths had been spread on the thick, wiry grass. There were several galvanized tubs filled with chunks of ice, around which were packed bottles of beer and soda. Some of the women held parasols. The cerulescent sky was cloudless and the sunlight came through the thick-leaved apple trees and dappled the grass with patches of light. Children ran about, and men sat in groups, smoking. I have often thought of how a talented and perceptive artist, a Georges Seurat, perhaps, might have created a superb *tableau vivant* of that scene, might have rendered it as a *danse macabre*, a choreography of the absurd, the grotesque spectacle of one race making a festive occasion of the tragedy of another. It was, in fact, a double tragedy: for the Indians, a personal one; for the white audience, the tragedy of their insensitivity and inhumanity.

When it grew dark, the Indians built a small bonfire, a *wuke*, which appeared to wink. My mother explained that the winking was caused by the *kalte*, which in such ceremonies is a slow, measured dance around a freshly built fire that symbolized *hiema*, the rising sun. The fire winked in the interval between passing dancers. The ululations and keening were steady now, and rhythmical to the introduction of a slow drum beat. In the darkness, the white folks gathered inside the arbor, through the sagging and latticed roof of which rhomboids of starry sky glittered. No one expressed sadness over the tragedy of First Brother and Third Brother. They talked of nice old Indians they had known. I had just passed my fourth birthday when I witnessed and experienced that afternoon and evening. It has remained a constant picture in my mind. If symbolism is discernible here in such a flagrant and unconscious acting out of racial callousness, surely it is to be found in that narrow lane, a barbed wire ribbon of demarcation between Indian and white five hundred years wide. And there is irony. The white folk in the orchard never considered their festive intrusion upon a tragedy to be thoughtless or callous. It was entertainment, the same as watching a parade. Years later I asked an old man who had been present if he did not, in hindsight, think it had been wrong and offensive to have a picnic to watch the Injuns ki-yi (in my uncle's immortal words). "No, no," he said with some asperity. "We was watchin' history. You don't see that sort of thing no more."

Well, you don't. Holding a picnic on the edge of someone else's grief *is* a bit rare.

And Third Brother and the Cousin? Third Brother was tried for manslaughter. But neither his court appointed attorney nor the prosecution could get anything more from him than, "HE got runned over," and a nervous laugh and shrug. The Cousin repeated Happy's words. "Got mean. Accident. Got in front of the car. Got runned over. Accident." Third Brother was sentenced to eighteen months in the county jail. Although I have not had access to the records, I do not believe he served the full term. He was soon back on the streets of Murphys. The Cousin was given three years probation. Happy was tried in absentia and sentenced to five years for manslaughter and for shooting at a duly formed posse, but without intent to kill, and for unlawful flight to avoid prosecution.

Years later I often went hunting with Third Brother. He

never mentioned his brother or the time spent in jail. He was a good hunting companion. He was always good natured. He was a resourceful woodsman. He hunted for food, not for sport. He still laughed his nervous laugh followed by the automatic shrug. He died of acute alcoholism. The Cousin's words come back: "They 'dint know what else to do but fight. It still seems like a dream. I kin still hear them screams and feel them bumps un'er the car. They wasn't even mad at each other." And later: "Maybe we was never here, never lived. If you write it down, we was here, we lived.

THREE

Aaron

My hometown, Murphys, was typical of the little Mother Lode mining camps of Northern California that had climaxed in the 1850s and 1860s, then aged gracefully into somnolent beauty. The great wounds inflicted by the miners—the nozzle-ripped hillsides, the frighteningly deep glory holes, the gashed and tunneled mountains—healed under the growth of manzanita and chaparral, of oak and of pine whose falling needles softened the harsh contours of rock piles and filled rutted roads into gentle depressions.

Like all western towns, Murphys had its corner store—cracker barrel, pot-bellied stove, and all—named for a turn in the road. It was an old stone building; chairs and benches were set out on the front porch where the old men sat of summer evenings, cooled by the tarweed-scented breezes that blew in from the irrigation ditches in the fields, and talked about the "early days." For history had, indeed, passed here, passed quickly and was gone, leaving a handful of old men scattered behind to keep its memory green.

In the late 1930s, when I was a boy, I would sit for hours in the evenings listening to stories of miners, teamsters, trappers, badmen and, best of all, of Indians. I would listen until long after dark when the voices were disembodied and floated about

TNDIAN "JIM

FIG 14. Indian Jim. Colorful and aggressive. Paid for a day's labor with a jug of wine. Drank it all and died. Courtesy Lottie Stephens.

so that I had trouble fixing face to voice. When the conversation lulled I would say, "Talk about Indians." They would: about the rancherias and roundhouses and Indian shacks, now long gone, about "buryin' grounds" and where they were, where Indian beads came from, and mortar rocks, about shooting and knifing scrapes, about the few old Indians who still lived there. And always the voices were edged with a contemptuous humor when they talked about Indians. Whatever an Indian's misfortune, it was reason enough to laugh.

One evening as I sat listening to the men, four old Indians shuffled past. They looked at us, craning their necks stiffly, fearfully, I thought. "There go your Injuns, Boy," an old man sneered. "Diggers! They're lower'n animals."

I learned a lot of history from the "old-timers," but I also inherited their prejudices, and I was respectful of my inheritance. Besides, those few shabby old Indians left hardly fitted my Chateaubriandesque(a French author, Vicomte Francois René de Chateaubriand, 1766–1848, who idealized theIndians)

visions of rivers and lakes and canoes and roached savages flit-
ting through deep forests, or my Zane Grey *Spirit of the Border*
sentimentalities of the feathered and noble savage. And while I
would like to think of myself as being regretful, even as a boy,
of my persecutions, and am tempted now to lay it entirely to
my inheritance and fear of being shamed by the other boys, I
was, nevertheless, as unremitting in my childish cruelty as the
next. I helped saw the undersides of boards the Indians put
down across streams that cut their path up over the mountains
to the acorn groves. I rump-shot their few scrub and rabbity
horses with BB-guns. And along with the others I screamed:
DIGGER! DIGGER! BLACK AS A NIGGER! at uncom-
prehending and demoralized old Indians who stood staring at
us in fright. They were too pathetically few in number to per-
mit themselves even the simple dignity of ignoring us.

I doubt that my humanity should ever have been aroused
had it not been for old Aaron and the death of his horse. Aaron
was almost certainly in his eighties. He slept in the manger of
an old barn and wore filthy cast-off clothing. He walked with
a bent-knee, foot-slapping shuffle, and his neck was so stiff he
could not turn to look in any direction without stopping. His
eyes were murky and unfathomable translucent pits in white
rheumy foam. He smelt like a wet dog. Aaron had never completely submitted to the white man. There was still fight in
him. If the boys teased him beyond endurance, he would reach
slowly into his pocket, pull out a knife, and with ominous de-
liberation open it and point the blade at them. They kept their
distance.

Aaron always kept a horse. But as long as I knew him he was
too old to ride. He led the horse, and he walked at a shuffling
trot, afraid it would walk over him. His eyes were frightened
and suspicious, and he would turn stiffly from side-to-side to
catch the horse out of the corner of his eye. He pastured the

animal wherever permitted. The day the horse was killed it was pastured in my uncle's field. He was a proud-cut, half wild, blue roan with a wall-eye, and when you approached, he would throw up his head and rumble threateningly deep in his barrel. Sometimes it would take Aaron an hour or more to catch him. He would shuffle slowly toward the horse, softly muttering "he, he, he," carrying a lasso which, on a lucky day, he was able to reach over the horse's head. More often, he had to rope the animal as it broke out of a fence corner, flicking out the rope and letting it go quickly if it settled over the neck. The horse would drag the rope a few yards and give up. Aaron would walk up slowly, pick up the end of the rope, and gather him in.

On this day, the horse was unusually wild. The old Indian had stopped me as I came down the lane from my uncle's house and asked me to help corner his horse. We worked it around and around the field, but each time it broke out of the corners, snorting wildly, wall-eye rolling, and running a kicking, flatulent run. We cornered him, finally, in a deep-weeded wedge of barbed wire fence. We did not know of the abandoned harrow that lay there covered, its teeth choked with foxtails and thistles. The roan broke away and Aaron flicked the rope. The noose fell short and whacked him on the neck, turning him, so that he raced through the deep weeds and drove his leg down through the harrow and somersaulted, screaming horribly, into the barbed wire fence, ripping the harrow up out of the grass and smashing the fence so that the wires snapped and whizzed back into quivering coils. The horse lay screaming, blowing blood from its flared and ripped nostrils. Its leg was nearly torn off. I did not see the entrails on the barbed wire until later. I heard Aaron yelling "Git gun, git gun." I ran to town, and a rancher drove me back and shot the horse.

We stood looking at the horse, saying nothing. Then, for the first time, I looked at Aaron. He was crying softly and rubbing his eyes with his knuckles. I am unable to describe my own feelings at that moment. I walked with the bent and defeated old Indian back to his barn, listening to the soft and incongruous crying. Without knowing why, I kept saying over and over

in my mind "digger, digger, black as a nigger," and "lower'n an animal." I watched him go inside where there was no one to talk to, none of his kind to understand his loss, only a dirty tack room with its strong horse smell and an empty manger to lie in, now not even a horse to hold to, to call friend, and give a man a reason for being. I am tempted now to find a parallel with *Huck Finn*. Certainly, Huck's amazement at discovering that blacks were human in Jim's tears was no greater than my own now. But Aaron and I rafted down no river, camped on no island, illuminated

FIG 15. Aaron, behind the barn he lived in— Murphys. Courtesy Bill Harper.

no social evils. And I waged no valiant and victorious struggle with my conscience. But I did feel a deep and abiding anger with myself for the unquestioning acceptance of the cruel and thoughtless prejudices of which I had been so childishly mindful. I never teased another Indian.

In time, Aaron got another horse. It was a scrubby hammerhead gelding, and I helped him break it, the Indian way, by letting the horse run endlessly in circles at the end of double lariats and finally throwing on the saddle and letting him run some more. When I'd at last mount up, he was too tired to walk. I stopped calling Aaron "Chief," too, and he stopped calling me "Chief" in return. It was Aaron and Chackie. In the summer of 1939, I took a job on a ranch driving a milk truck, and unknown to the rancher, I left two quarts a day at Aaron's barn. "You goot poy, Chackie," he would say softly. It was enough for me.

Aaron showed me "Injun medicine" which turned out, disappointingly, to be patches of pale green wild sage that grew near the ranch where I worked. I had heard so much about miraculous Indian curatives I was expecting something magic and mysterious, some exotic root, perhaps, or crushed oak balls. When he took me to the patches, we went in great secrecy, lying beside the trail and watching to see that we were not followed. He had an iron kettle cached near by, a big spoon, and a dipper, and in a hidden clearing by a log, there was a circle of rocks with an old iron grill set across it. This was where he boiled sage leaves and concocted his medicine, a foul-tasting brew that was like a liquid evisceration. I tasted it once. I'd have to be dying to taste it again.

One morning in the early fall, I stopped with the milk and found Aaron outside, leaning against the barn, a blanket over his head and shoulders.

"Aaron," I said. "You sick?"

"Sick," he replied, inside the blanket.

"Get doctor," I said, starting for the truck.

"No," he said, still under the blanket.

"Get doctor," I repeated.

"No. Go medicine." He walked slowly to the truck, and I helped him in.

"Doctor," I said again, starting the motor.

"No. Go medicine. *Now.*"

He kept the blanket over his head and said nothing more. By driving through a back field and over an old wagon road, I was able to get within a hundred yards or so of the medicine patch.

I helped him walk to the clearing, and he sat on the log. I gathered wood and pine cones and got the fire going under the grill. Then I ran to the creek and filled the kettle and set it on the grill. I filled the kettle with sage leaves, and they floated in circles as the water began to boil.

When the steam commenced to rise, he moved forward and took the blanket off. He had had a stroke. His face was twisted hideously, his nose pulled taut as a bowstring to the left, the left eye stretched bloodily down to the corner of the mouth that twisted up to meet it. He leaned forward with his face in the steam. I brought up a dipperful of brew, but he shook his head. I let the dipper slide into the kettle where he could reach it. He motioned for the blanket, and I draped it over his head. The steam came up inside, and I caught the stench of dirty woolens. I gathered a pile of wood so he could reach it and drove back to town.

Along the route I kept reporting what had happened. No one was interested. One old-timer said, "Hell, he'll be all right. Them Injuns is tougher'n hog-gut."

That night I grabbed some food and a bucket and hurried back to Aaron. I expected to find him dead, but he was still sitting on the log, under the blanket, and now he was chanting softly. Having read too deeply of Natty Bumppo and of Custer, I assumed it was his "death song." The fire was still going, and I could see that he had put on more wood. The dipper was still in the kettle. I put my hand on his shoulder. "Eat?" I asked. He did not answer. He kept chanting. I brought more water and leaves to the kettle and piled up fresh wood. Then I put down the food and left.

Next morning I left an hour early to look in on him. He was still on the log, still under the blanket, still chanting softly. He had not touched his food, but he had used most of the wood, and the dipper was lying against the log. He had drunk.

The third and fourth days were the same, and the fifth. I gathered wood, carried water, and brought food, which he did not touch. I had not seen his face again. On the sixth day, I got the shock of my life. I hurried up to find him sitting on the log grinning; his face was normal except for a slight twist to the nose. He had eaten all the food.

"Hello, Chackie," he said.

"How you feel?" I replied.

"Goot. Injun medicine plenty goot."

"Yes," I said, and I meant it. "Take you home now?"

"No. Go bimeby, mebbeso two, mebbeso t'ree day."

He went in two. In twelve days, he was leading his horse. No one was surprised. An old man who had spent his life among the Indians said, "They got a medicine, Boy, better'n anything we got. I wish I knew what it is."

Many years later, I asked my mother, who was born and raised on her father's ranch a quarter of a mile from a rancheria, what she thought of Aaron's recovery. She shrugged. Not one to exaggerate, she told me the story of my grandfather, W. H. Saunders. He had been kicked on the back of the hand by a calf. A hard, black lump, about an inch high, formed and continued to grow. Dr. George Pache in Angles Camp was baffled, and my grandfather was afraid he would lose his hand. Then an Indian who was haying for grandfather noticed the hand and asked about it. He looked at it closely, felt it, and said, "I fix." He went to his shack and came back with a can of salve. He rubbed it on the growth, insisting on applying it himself, and a week later the growth was gone. Poor old "Doc" Pache. He drove up in his buckboard and pleaded with the Indian for the ingredients, appealed to his humanitarian instincts, and, as a last resort, offered him twenty-five dollars cash. It was no sale.

Aaron took sick in his barn, during the Second World War.

There was no one to take him to his medicine patch, no one to fill his kettle with water and boil the wild sage. He was hauled off to the county hospital in San Andreas. They cut his dirty clothes off and put him in a tubfull of hot water. He died in the tub. When I asked an old-timer how Aaron died, he laughed. "Took him to the hospital, gave him a bath, and it killed him. With all that dirt scraped off, nothing left to hold him up." Another said, "When they wiped the puss out of his eyes, and he got a look at the civilized world, he died of fright."

Aaron is buried in Murphys' Protestant Cemetery. The Catholics did not want a pagan in their consecrated earth. Aaron was born on the hill where the Catholic church now stands. He showed me the sight. His grave is in a small grove of pines on the eastern side of Buena Vista Cemetery Hill. The first rays of the morning sun scatter bright shards of light through the pines and across his grave. He is not buried, as he should have been, facing the rising sun. Aaron's grave marker, like Walker's, is an incised pauper's slab on which someone managed to misspell his name:

ARON
THE INDIAN

But it doesn't matter. Aaron wasn't his real name anyway. And at least the marker says "Indian."

Perhaps, in the passage of time, along with today's emphasis on "Indianness," I have tended to idealize Aaron. But I cannot help thinking of him as waging an almost solitary struggle to retain something of himself, of his tradition and identity, however conscious or unconscious—or instinctive—that struggle might have been. He lived in his barn among his personal trappings, he carried a *chomuck* sack, but he did not beg—and what was offered he accepted with quiet dignity. He made hidden camps in the woods and lived out during good weather. He kept his horse even though he was too old to ride, and he was his own ministrant when ill, practicing pure "Injun medicine." His compromises were few; he suffered the white man far more than the white man suffered him.

FOUR

Mary

Aaron was not the only Miwok Indian to hold to something of himself, to his past and to his pride. An old "squaw" called Mary (no one knew her real name; she probably did not remember it herself) who, though compromised and cynically debauched by the white man, never surrendered her fierce pride and spirit. Mary was, as one old-timer who ought to have known put it, "Sure as hell no Minnehaha." Born in Murphys around 1850, Mary was a wild and lusty young Indian woman whose morals were simply those of the white men around her. She remembered the red-shirted miners swarming up and down the streams with their clanking gold pans and picks. And from them she acquired both a hair-raising (though otherwise limited) vocabulary and the absolute conviction of the way in which she must conduct her life: that her spiritual and physical survival meant meeting the white man on his own profane and exploitive level. She would not be used without using. She learned that lusty old Anglo-Saxon word in both its literal meaning and epithetic intent, and she used it with diabolical and humiliating skill. The white man's profanity became Mary's weapon.

As she grew older, she drank anything and as much as she could get hold of, usually cheap red wine, and when the drinking of it made her sick, she would vomit without self-consciousness wherever she chanced to be; and she usually chanced to be in a public place and in the presence of a white audience. "SOHNAWAHBEECH!" she would exclaim, laughing and patting her big stomach and belching loudly. "Feel BETTAH now." The more sorely wounded the delicate sensibilities of the whites about her, the louder she laughed. When she was young, I am told, she danced the *kalte* (dance) around the big orange bonfires, the *wuke*, in the Rocky Hill Roundhouse. She danced it with wild and uninhibited abandon, boldly and sinuously intruding on the ranks of the male dancers and holding close to the showering flames, head back and face glistening, long black hair swinging against her shoulders, her piercing ululations rising above the chanting of the men and the *muli-ni*, the singing of the women in the outer circle.

Mary prostituted herself freely and without shame, even into very old age. Her price was whatever the traffic would bear and generally equated with time, place, and sense of urgency. But she never permitted herself to be degraded. She moved evenly with her white customer. She was always what he was, never less. Often she was much more. Mary was a sentient being with a proud sense of a lost history and a free way of life. But she had none of the Indian illusions that some sort of spiritual or cosmic force would one day drive the white men from Indian land. She was irrevocably linked to the white man and to what was now clearly his world. She would always be scorned and loathed by white women to whom she had become the repulsive and unfathomable symbol of the degradation, the reality of the true sexual beings of their men. Mary

FIG 16. Mary, unknown, and Walker. (Only
picture of Mary)—Murphys. Courtesy Bill
Harper.

understood these things. There was left to her only the strong
will to live and the determination to hold to her pride and
dignity. And when her pride and dignity were threatened, she
played the white men and women off against each other with
barbaric skill.

The white men were the prostitutes, really. They expended
themselves over the fat and wrinkled old body. They averted
their eyes from the red wine stains in the deep mouth wrinkles
and the black, funereal stumps of teeth. If Mary did not like a
customer, she would smile her black malicious smile and croon,
"You no like KEES Mary, HONNEEE?" But if the price were
right, a silver dollar, usually, and the approach respectful, and
whether the place was inside a barn or back of it, or in the long,

crushed grass of a field or behind a bush by the roadside, Mary walked to it with simple and quiet dignity, not after the fashion of the "squaws" who slunk reticently and fearfully to their assignations as if to their executions. She was known to settle for a quarter, but the men who made the offer never made it again, nor did they ever forget or quite recover from the experience. She would snatch the quarter and scream, "SOHNA-WAHBEECH, CHEAP GOTTAM BAWSTD. You like FOKUM, fokum like AHNIMAL." She would drop, cursing, to her hands and knees, flip up her long black skirt, hump her big sagging and wrinkled buttocks up and down and grunt, "Uh, Uh, Uh, fokum like wan TCUKU (dog). "She'd gyrate that big fat ass of hern' in a figger eight," one old-timer said, still shaking his head in awe forty-odd years later. "You'd see that big black ass rollin' an' humpin' and likely she'd fart, too, and you didn't want none of it, but she'd allus keep the two-bits."

Once Mary lived with Walker in his *kotca* (his cabin) on the hill. She kept his cabin clean, and she cooked whatever the old man was able to beg. She pounded acorns into meal in the mortar basins on the ledge below the cabin and leached out the tannic acid in the ice-cold spring that bubbled up through the roots of a clump of blue-needled Digger pines. She made acorn bread and *hartoli* (soup), and *nupa* (mush). But when Walker became infirm and too old to beg food, Mary left him for a "squaw-man" who lived in a shack near Douglas Flat. It was not a matter of desertion, of cruelty, or of being "uncivilized," as the white folks said. Walker's time had come. He could no longer care for his woman. To the Indians, all life forms were volatile and capable of becoming something else. To survive, Mary would be a white man's woman. Walker understood. He would wait the howling summons of *oletcu* (the coyote) who created the Miwok people and would bear his spirit to the next world. The coyote was both a yapping, earth-bound hunter whose fur was valuable, and a spirit-god. Nature responded only to the law of volatility.

When Mary visited Indian friends who lived in the hills around Murphys, she did not slip timidly across the back fields or through the woods as the other Indian women did. She walked right through town, and though she hated and feared the automobile, the *too-KOO-loo-loo*, as something both unnatural and intrusive, she always strutted defiantly down the middle of the road. When she heard a car approaching, she would stand off the road, hold her skirts up and thrust her mons obscenely forward and backward, scream curses, and jab her middle finger up and down. She had learned the gesture from the white man. Strangers chancing to drive by her were profoundly shocked. Often they would report a "crazy old Indian woman" out on the road. One man blamed Mary because he drove his car into a tree watching her do humps and thrusts by the roadside. He said that while the blood ran down his face from a broken nose, Mary danced and hooted with laughter. Some of the older boys drove back and forth past her to watch her "perform." When they honked their horns, Mary would grab up rocks and rush screaming at their cars. Once a boy killed his motor. Before he could get the car started, Mary smashed his windshield. When some young men drove past her to show-off for their girl friends, Mary slowly, even majestically, raised her skirts, squatted, and relieved herself. The young men and their girls drove quickly away to Mary's hooting cackle and viciously stabbing finger. Mary considered the automobile to be a great inconvenience. "No GOTTAM GOOT," too-KOO-loo-loo," she would exclaim. She would accept a ride from no one.

I met Mary, when I was seven years old and two years before she died. At the time, my family lived in a small house that abutted a corral. There was a big barn in the corral, and between the barn and our house, three towering and massive water oaks stood in a rough semicircle. In the spring, the sap rose, and the three oaks were gravid with acorns. One of the oaks, the largest one, threw out a thick, canescent root that flattened bench-like along its top before it plunged back into the earth. The root had been a seating place for cattlemen and teamsters since the 1870s. Its flat surface was worn smooth. In the fall, the sun came through the thinning red leaves and lay in yellow patches on the brown-jacketed acorns that now covered the ground. I picked the acorns up in a bucket and filled burlap sacks. I sold them to a hog farmer for a dollar a sack. One glittering October morning after a quick, fresh rain, I was picking up acorns. The oaks were filled with birds. The rain droplets sparkled on the branches. When the birds hopped about, the droplets showered down, prismatically rainbowed in the bright, leaf-filtered sunlight. I heard Mary coming before I saw her. She was humming that peculiar, resonating sound the Miwok's used to announce their presence. They did not like taking white people by surprise. Mary was walking down the middle of the road. When she saw me, she turned into the corral. She walked slowly and heavily. She was smiling when she came up, and she knew my name. "Hello, Chackie," she said. "You goot boy. Work. Pick up *wilisa*."

"What?" I said, surprised.

"*Wilisa*." She stooped slowly and scooped up a handful of acorns. "*Wilisa*," she said, holding out the acorns. Her palms were white. "You say—*wilisa*."

"*Wilisa*," I said.

"Goot."

She walked to the flat root and sat down. She sighed. "Christ, I *strocco* [tired]." She patted the root and smiled. "You come sit Mary."

I sat by her. She was very fat. She wore a long black skirt and a gray blouse. Her hair was thick and heavy. It was gray in places and very black in others. Her face was flat-browed and seamed with deep wrinkles, a face distilled to its eternal essence. Her mouth was very wide and curved down at the corners. Her upper lip and the corners of her mouth were lined with wrinkles. Her teeth were black and decayed stumps. Her fingers were long and dry looking, like brittle sticks, but her eyes were very bright and when she smiled, they shone. There was no rheum in them. She was very nice. She smiled at me.

"You like talk Enjun, Chackie?"

"Yes," I said. I had heard a tall, lean cattleman speak the language to two Indians who worked for him. He sounded very important.

Mary put her hand on the tree trunk. "*Leka* [tree]" she said. "You say—*leka*."

"*Leka*," I said.

"Goot." She looked up in the oak and pointed to a bright, orange and buff and black-spotted bird, hooked into the tree trunk by ice-tong claws and braced against its stiff tail.

"*Tiwaiu* [yellowhammer]. You say—*tiwaiu*."

"*Tiwaiu*," I answered.

"Goot." She pointed to a woodpecker edging his way up the tree trunk, his drumming red-head flashing in the sunlight. "*Palatata*. You say—*palatata*."

"*Palatata*," I said.

She pointed to a blue jay hopping through the branches and shaking down droplets of dew. "*Taite*. You say—*taite*."

"*Taite*," I repeated. She picked up a rock and held it out. "*Sawa*. You say—*sawa*."

"*Sawa*," I said.

"Plenty goot," she said. "Plenty goot today."

She sat quietly. She hummed a little. She smiled at me and patted me and called me "Goot poy." When she left, she said,

"Be back bimeby. Talk more Enjun. Learn." She walked heavily out into the middle of the road. Then she turned and walked down the white line.

I cannot recall how many times I saw Mary over the last two years of her life. I am satisfied it was between thirty and forty times. If I were not in the corral or playing in the barn when she came, she sat out on the flat root humming louder and louder until I heard her and came running. I looked forward to her visits. I worried about her. I was afraid she would be run down by a car. She always smiled when she saw me. Her smile was deep and broad. Her black eyes gleamed and sparkled with intelligent humor. Her smile transcended her black stumps of teeth.

I know that Mary was a natural teacher. Each time she returned, I was expected to remember the names and words she taught me. She would point silently to the blue jay.

"Taite," I would say. She would nod and smile. Often she corrected my accent or pronunciation. In turn, she pointed to each object or creature whose designation or name she had taught me before. When I remembered them all, she would put her arm around me and smile and pat my shoulder and say, "Goot poy. Talk Enjun GOOT, bimeby."

Her visits with me over the months grew more and more maternal. She patted me more often. When we sat on the oak root, she sometimes taught me words with her arm around my shoulder. She was very serious. She wanted me to learn her language. Mary and I expanded our small universe. We took short walks in the fields and along the banks of a stream. She no longer repeated Indian words and said, "You say." She pointed to the stream. "*Wakalu*," she said.

"*Wakalu*," I repeated.

She stooped slowly and heavily and dipped up a handful of water and let it run through her fingers. "*Kiku*."

"*Kiku*," I answered. A small frog splashed into the stream.

"*Wataksaiyi*," she said, pointing.

"*Wataksaiyi*," I said.

Where the stream pooled darkly under the roots of a big white oak, tiny minnows swam in and out of slanting, broken shafts of sunlight. Mary peered into the pool. She pointed. "*Lapisaiyu*," she said.

"*Lapisaiyu*," I repeated.

Mary's English (aside from profanity, which she never used around me) was considerably less than rudimentary. She learned what she needed to learn to survive and no more. Except for *hiema* (the sun) we had to wait for changes in the weather before she could put Indian names to other extra-terrestrial phenomena. One morning Mary suddenly pointed excitedly to the sky. A thin, faintly white rind of moon hung limply over the hills. "*Kome*," she said, smiling. "*Kome*."

"*Kome*," I repeated.

Another time it began to rain. She held out her hands. "*Nuka*."

"*Nuka*," I responded obediently.

We went into the barn and stood watching the rain. When a clap of thunder rolled in from the hills, she cupped her ear, then clapped her hands and laughed.

"*TiMEle*," she said.

"*Timele*," I repeated.

"No! *TiMEle*."

"*TiMEle*," I corrected myself.

"GOOT!" She laughed and patted me. I took her hand. She held my hand firmly until she left.

I awakened one morning to a fresh snow. It seldom snowed in Murphys. I hurried out to the barnyard. The electric wires were fuzzed-out and sagging with snow. The oaks were heavily laden. Bluebirds sat in dark huddled rows on the wires. They puffed their feathers out against the cold. The irregular contours of the barn were smooth under the snow's white sheath. Back of the barn I found a fox track. The fox had trotted past the barn door, stopped to sniff at the urine-yellowed snow where the cows had passed in and out of the barn, then headed for the hen house. I was tracking the fox when Mary appeared. She was not humming. Her feet crunched in the dry powder. She wore a heavy, brown man's coat. It was frayed at the shoulders. There was a wool scarf over her head. The scarf was lightly dusted with snow. Mary had not come by the road. She had crossed the fields from her cabin near Douglas Flat. She was walking much faster than usual. She was cold. Her breath plumed in the freezing air. She smiled quickly and said, "Hello Chackie." She clutched her coat from the inside. It had no buttons. She scuffed the snow with a foot. Then she bent slowly and heavily and scooped up a handful and held it out. It was very white in her hand.

"*Kela*," she said. "*Kela*."

"*Hu* [yes]," I answered. "*Kela*"

"*Kudji. Kudji* [good, good]. Talk Enjun GOOT." She stood quietly, looking at me as if a certain moment had come and passed too quickly, as if something more needed to be said or done. Then without impulse, without hurry, she put her arms around me and held me tight. I smelt the strong Indian smell of her. She whispered, "Goot poy." She brushed her hand over my hair and released me. I wanted her to hold me longer. There were tears in her eyes. I thought they were from the cold. Then she turned and walked away. Her tracks were big and dark in the snow. For some reason, her tracks did not seem to take her away. I thought of the tracks then as a line flowing with her energy, a line that drew us together and held us. Mary stopped on the far edge of the field. She stood for a moment, dark and doll-like in the distance, luminously accentuated by the black clouds lowering against the bright snow. It had begun to snow again. I waved. She did not wave back. Indians rarely wave. She stood for a moment, then turned and disappeared into the swirling flakes. I looked up. The snowflakes were dark and peppery in the thin light. I suddenly felt very lonely. I watched Mary's tracks filling with the new snow as nature softly recomposed itself, blotting out the moments past, the little journey taken. It came over me slowly that Mary had walked six miles to tell me the Indian word for snow. "*Kela*," I said to myself. "*Kela. Kela. Kela.*"

I do not remember the last time I saw Mary. Her last three or four visits run together in my mind. She was completely absorbed in teaching me the words and meaning to a song. She wanted me to sing with her. I sensed that the song was very important to her. She did not smile or laugh those last three or four days. She would sit on the oak root and begin humming. Her eyes were closed. Then she began to sing. She kept her hand on my shoulder. Her voice was husky and low. There was a melody to the song. It was not a chant.

"*Muli-ni* [sing]," she said. I knew the words, and I sang with her:

> Chepalali wooxum, luti-ti nana-ti
> Chepalali wooxum, luti osa-ti
> Chepalali wooxum, luti allene-k
> Chepalali wooxum, sh-we
> Nitchee wan, nitchee wan, uya-ti, allene-k
> Chepalali wooxum, saiye uya-ti
> Chepalali wooxum, hisum hana-ti
> Hana-ti, hana-ti, hana-ti ch-wooxum, ch-we
> Honanne Hisum, Honanne Hisum
> Tupuila hisum, Tupuila hisum
> Hana-ti yenna-ni.

A number of the words have no exact counterpart in English, but I understood that the song was the story of an Indian boy and an Indian girl. The boy and the girl were in love. The girl was raped or seduced by an older white man. The boy went into the mountains and killed himself by taking poison. I do not recall when it came to me that the girl was Mary.

The old-timers, those "sturdy pioneers" of history and fiction, told dozens of stories about Mary, most of them crude and tasteless, some grimly humorous. As far as history is concerned, they would hardly be worthy of recording if it were not for the pervasive overtones of degradation, along with Mary's heroic and often brutal struggle to survive with her pride and spirit whole. The stories are historical extrapolations. I heard them repeated over and over. I hated the stories then. I am less than philosophic about them now.

One day, sometime in 1905, a story goes, and when Mary was about fifty-five, she charged into a general store, and whacking the dirt and loose grass from her long black skirt, told the startled storekeeper at the top of her voice and with an appalling variety of gestures, that his two sons had met her in the woods and had done the obvious. It was not a question of outraged morality: "No pay," she shouted. "GOTTAM SOHNAWAHBEECHES go Uh, Uh, Uh, like wan EPLALI [rabbit], go WHEEEE, WHEEEE, WHEEEE." She squealed the rabbits' orgasmic scream in the stunned merchant's face and thrust her pelvis forward in jerks and rolled her hips obscenely and grunted, "Uh, Uh, Uh. No Pay! YOU pay."

Four or five men sat at a card table in a back corner. They laughed. Mary whirled, "Foke you, Charlie," she hissed (Mary called all white men "Charlie." As far as I know, I am the only white male she called by name.) The men laughed. The merchant looked about nervously.

"How much," he asked, in a low voice.

"Fi' dolla."

"NO. Too much."

"Tell you WIFE, SOHNAWAHBEECH," Mary yelled. "See Sher'f. Have 'rest gottam poys, put CHAIL. You beeg BULLSHIT!"

Mary flung around to go. The merchant rang up No Sale. Mary turned, grinning a mean, wine-stained grin. The merchant held out a bill. Mary snatched the bill and stuffed it in a pocket. She laughed. One of the men at the card table called, "Hey Mary. You like fokum?" Mary walked over to the table. She grinned and leaned forward and put her hands on her hips. She was rich now and expansive.

"Not you, Charlieee," she crooned. She thrust out her pelvis. "You no gottam goot. Got LEETLE wan, dees way." She held her thumb and forefinger an inch apart. "No can FEEL, like wan leetle poy."

The men laughed. One said, "I heard you wasn't too well fixed, Charliee."

"Git on out. Git," Charlie said to Mary. "Goddam dirty old squaw. GIT!"

"Foke you, Charlieeee," Mary sang. "You no fokeing goot. Got wan leetle PETAH, dees way." She held up her fingers again. Then she walked out the door, hooting with laughter. She heard "Charlie" cursing back in the store. The merchant stared after her from behind the No Sale on the register.

There were stories of Mary lying in the musty hay of an old barn surrounded by very young men, her skirts pulled up past the wrinkled old belly, past the pendulous breasts that flattened into the hay on either side of her body, the insides of her thighs and the sparse pubic hair glazed and stiff with the effulgence of premature ejaculations and clumsy and misdirected efforts of penetration. The boys got no manual help or guidance from Mary. Outside the barn, four or five smirking louts lagged about, awaiting their turns in the hay. It was said that Mary had de-flowered more young men and caused more divorces and given more doses of clap than any other single individual in the whole of the United States. It was said that Mary never participated in the sex act. It was said that she lay still and stared into the face of her partner with black angry eyes. It was said that she threatened to kill anyone who suggested oral sex.

There is the story of Mary tracked across a light snow by four young boys barely in their teens. Mary's squaw-man lay sick in his cabin. She had gone into the woods to gather wild sage and *kit kit dizze* (colloquially known as "mountain mis-ery") for medicine. The boys offered her fifty cents each. Mary stood quietly studying the boys. There was no trace of the unmistakable lineaments of young manhood in the white, downy faces. She shook her head.

"NO," she told them. "Too yong poys. No GOOT yong poys. Go MAMAS."

The boys persisted. They held their money out.

"NO," Mary said. "No GOOT. *Kela* too cold 'po ASSHOLE!"

Even with the possibility of sex fused with such crude real-ity, the boys stood their ground, holding out their fifty-cent pieces, their libidinous expectations still intact. Mary grinned her black grin, slowly raised her skirts, squatted, and relieved herself in hissing yellow spurts that sizzled into the snow. Steam rose around her great dark buttocks. Revolted, the boys stumbled off through the trees. They had not succeeded in casting off their virginity, but they had tasted their sexual be-ings. They could hear Mary laughing back in the woods. From the way they told the story in later years, they had been little heroes that day. They had disdained a filthy old squaw who pissed in the snow.

One of Mary's steadiest customers was a retired merchant

and Murphys' "peeping Tom." The Merchant was well into his eighties, but it was said that he was twenty-five from the waist down. A long, red-wattled neck thrust out from his hunched and rounded shoulders. His head was bald and very red on top and fringed with white hair. His eyes were light blue and watery and expressionless, and they did not align properly when refracted behind thick-lensed, rimless spectacles. He wore a short, bristly mustache that twitched involuntarily. But he walked with the easy springy step of a man a fraction of his age. He could run like a sprinter. At one time or another, the glint of spectacles, the twitchy white mustache, and the flash of his bald pate were glimpsed at nearly every bedroom window in town. He had seen more than half the women in Murphys naked. He had probably seen many of them in coition. He was seen peeping through the willows at the swimming hole, watching the girls undress. He had been chased into the dark by husbands and young men. No one could catch him. When he was accosted later, he would peer watery-eyed through his glasses and say, "You have the wrong man." The men threatened to beat him. No one did. He was too old. Everyone hated him. But no one was absolutely certain he was really the man. Some thought it was a young man with a mask.

One day some boys spotted the Merchant walking down the dirt sidewalk that ran in front of the dancehall and past a cluster of old barns. Mary waddled up the center of the road from the opposite direction, rocking from side to side like an old ship at its moorings. Their meeting appeared accidental. Mary angled off the road. The Merchant stopped and seemed to josh casually and briefly with her. But the boys saw something pass between them, something that flashed in the bright sunlight. Mary nodded. The Merchant continued down the sidewalk. Mary ambled slowly up the walk. Two barns stood next to the dancehall. There was a narrow passage-way between the barns that opened onto a flat area below the dancehall. The flat sprouted a forest of blue limestones that had been unearthed in twisted forms and shapes by the nozzle-blasts of the great hydraulic hoses of the Forty-Niners. Beyond the flat, Murphys Creek rushed through willowed tunnels and under an old wooden bridge; and across the creek was Jungle Park, a tangled labyrinth of wild blackberry vines through which trails had been trampled, connecting several large, grassy clearings shadowed under a graceful line of tall willows. Jungle Park was Murphys picnic spot.

Mary stopped in front of the barns. She looked slowly about

FIG 17. Unknown Indian woman—Rocky Hill, Murphys. Courtesy Bill Harper.

her. Then she moved into the passage-way. The boys intuited a rendezvous with the Merchant. They waited a few moments, then slipped through the passage-way and peered out. Mary had crossed the flat and was standing between an old red barn and a sheltering circle of limestones. The boys crawled to within fifty feet of her and lay in a little limestone-rimmed hollow. Presently the Merchant appeared. He had walked down the main street, turned into the dirt road between Bob's Inn and the old Sperry Hotel, and circled back to the flat. Now he walked his springy walk down to the bridge. He stood, pretending to study the water. He bent over and thoughtfully examined the wooden struts that braced the bridge against its length. He shook the railing. He bent his knees and bounced up and down to test its play. All the while he looked slowly and carefully about. Seeing no one, he walked quickly through the limestones to Mary. They spoke briefly. He bent over and cleared a spot on the ground. The boys saw Mary hoist her skirts and disappear down behind the rocks. The Merchant looked around, then dropped to his knees. The boys could see his bald head above the limestones.

At that moment, the boys sprang up and slammed rocks at the red wall of the barn. The rocks hammered against the barn like rifle shots above the Merchant's head. The Merchant popped up like a jack-in-the-box. He stood facing the boys, head up and mustache twitching, the suddenly defunct member in his left hand, the other raised, palm out, in solemn and majestic command: "Halt," he shouted. "You have the wrong man!" Then he turned and fled like a deer through the limestones and across the bridge into Jungle Park.

The boys walked over to Mary. They were laughing. Mary still lay on the ground, her skirts peeled up to the wrinkled belly. "SOHNAWAHBEECH," She said, bewildered. "Where he GO?" The boys pointed to Jungle Park. "SOHNA-

WAHBEECH. Like wan *EPLALI*." She still lay there "like an old skinned bear," as one boy said. The boys wondered about the bare spots in her pubic hair and the sheened insides of her thighs. The old-timers told them later the bare spots were where the hair was rubbed off by young boys like themselves missing the mark, and the inner thighs were worn smooth by overalls scraping up and down between them.

The boys helped Mary up. She began to laugh. "SOHNAWAHBEECH!" She held out a silver dollar. "I got dolla, he no FOKUM!" She threw back her head and slapped her big hips and laughed. She walked slowly toward the passage-way between the barns. She was still laughing and shaking her head. She held the silver dollar in her hand.

Of course, the story *is* bawdily humorous. The spectacle of the old man standing, hand up-raised, shouting, "You have the wrong man," and in the full glory of his flaccidity, has titillated three generations of Murphys' citizens. One man who had twice glimpsed the Merchant's face at his bedroom window exclaimed angrily, and with an innocent choice of words, "Now that old bastard really stands exposed." Murphys relished the story. There was no longer any doubt that the Merchant was its peeping Tom. It was hardly a historic event. But there is a follow-up story. Only two men in Murphys knew about it, and they were both pledged to secrecy by the Merchant's family. In their great age and after all parties were dead, the men, one a minor business man, the other a coroner's helper, told me the story. But the first part of the story came from Mary.

No one, of course, could divine the Merchant's thoughts and emotions as he raced that day through the brambles of Jungle Park and on into the woods beyond. He must have known that everyone in Murphys would now know for certain that he was their peeping Tom. Perhaps he cursed himself for stupidly shouting "You have the wrong man." Perhaps he burned with rage, and perhaps he was crazy. Whatever his reason, or reasons, the Merchant waylaid Mary that evening as she walked through a thick grove of live oaks midway between Murphys and Douglas Flat. Mary told the story later: "He PLENTY *saiye, kawune-ni* [bad, shout]. Want fokum." Mary tried to comply, to honor her paid commitment of the morning. But whether from the humiliating shock of the rocky interruption of his earthy coition, along with the foolish shouting of his stock phrase and his guilty flight, or from old age, or from all of these, the old satyr apparently suffered an attack of impotency. "No could DO," Mary said. "Like DEES." She waggled a limp forefinger. "Plenty *saiye*. Cuss. Want DOLLA back. No give. He hit (she gestured with her arm) *hana, suta, huku*, (head, eye, nose), take dolla."

Two days later Mary told her story to a deputy sheriff. The deputy laughed and threatened to arrest her for prostitution. She told the story to men in Murphys. She showed them her swollen nose and blackened eye. The men laughed. They believed Mary. So the lusty old Merchant was impotent. Well, that was a good one. But they could understand how he felt.

A little over a year later the business man stepped into his backyard one morning and found the Merchant lying dead under the bedroom window. He lay in a fetal position. He died as he had lived. The business man was angry. The dirty old bastard, he said to himself. He started to go for the constable. Then he thought of the Merchant's wife and family. The Merchant's wife was a lovely and refined woman. She had lived reclusively for years against the humiliating stories of her husband's sick and persistent voyeurism. Two sons and a daughter also lived in Murphys. The business man decided to go to the family before reporting the body to the constable. The family accepted the news in silence and without surprise. They proposed a conspiracy: The sons would pick up the body and haul it a half mile out on a back road and leave it at a designated spot. The business man would then "find" the body and report it to the constable.

All went as planned. The constable called the coroner, and the coroner came and examined the body. It bore no marks of violence. "Heart attack," the coroner said. "Old age." There was no autopsy or inquest. The Merchant was quickly buried on Cemetery Hill. The sons dug the grave. There were no services. Only the family and the young coroner's helper, whose presence was required by law, attended the burial. One of the sons stood at the cemetery gate and allowed no one else to enter. "We don't want the curious," he said. The mother and daughter huddled under the pines at the graveside. There was no officiating minister. The coroner's helper and the other son tied ropes around the coffin and kicked away the cross-pieces. Just as the coffin was lowered into the earth, Mary lumbered out of the pines. She had come to Cemetery Hill early that morning and waited in the pines. She stood by the grave a moment. Then she tossed something into the grave that landed with a ringing thud on the coffin. She turned and walked back through the pines. Before she passed out of earshot, she threw back her head and laughed. The coroner's helper looked into the grave. A silver dollar lay in the dirt where it had rolled, next to the coffin.

Given a life-time of peripatetic prostitution which began, literally, with her early youth, along with the very remote possibility that her random customers carried around condoms against a chance meeting, and the fact that pessaries were unknown even to most white women in the nineteenth century, it is remarkable that Mary did not produce several generations of mixed-blood children. As far as is known, unless she aborted herself or practiced some arcane method of birth control, she was made pregnant only once. Sometime between 1895 and

1900, when she was well past the normal child-bearing age, Mary bore a man-child to an itinerant Black man who appeared briefly in Murphys, then drifted on. "Took a wandering nigger to knock the old gal up," and old-timer said gracelessly. Mary named her son William, "like he papa." She was especially proud of him, the more so, perhaps, because he came along, like a good omen, late in her life. She called him "My Weelie Poy." Almost nothing is known of William's early life. He has been described as a shy, curly-haired little boy who walked everywhere with his mother, clinging silently to her long, black skirts. One winter afternoon, the story goes, Mary stopped at the Corner Store in Murphys. Little William stood timidly behind her, his hands enfolded tightly in her skirts. A group of men sat around a cherry-red stove. William kept his mother between himself and the men. Now and again he peeped around Mary's hips. It was cold in the thick-walled store. Mary moved close to the stove. One of the men leaned forward.

"What you doin' back there Nigger Bill," he said gruffly.

Mary whirled on the man. "Why you call heem NEEGER BEEL? SOHNAWAHBEECH, you. You see he papa FOKE me? My Weelie Poy GOOT poy, send SooNOrah POOKS LEARN [Sonora, books learn]."

From that moment on, though, William was known as Nigger Bill. Inexplicably, he was just as often called Nigger Bob. No one thought of his Indian blood. "A drop of nigger blood, makes a nigger baby," the people of Murphys said.

Bill did not go to school in Sonora. No one could recall when he left his mother and moved to Murphys. My first recollection of Nigger Bill was of a man in his thirties. He was very dark. He teeth were blackened stumps, like his mother's. I never saw him without a hat. Except for his rather thin, high-bridged nose, his features were Negroid. But his negritude was not of the Amos 'n' Andy sort, who at that time held the people of Murphys in near hypnotic thrall. Bill's mannerisms were Indian. He was quiet. In a group, he stood or sat back, just outside the human periphery, quietly watching and listening. He spoke good English. He did not volunteer conversation. He laughed often. His laugh was light and warm. Good humor flickered in his eyes and at the corners of his mouth. I doubt that many men existed so tragically and irrevocably on the nether side of humanity. Only a venerable cliché seems to suffice here: Bill was "neither fish, nor fowl." The Indians rejected him. The whites neither persecuted nor humiliated him. It might have been easier for him if they had. It would at least have given him definition, might even have taken some measure of the man. He was not ignored. He was spoken to and talked to with the arrogant courtesy one gives to a sub-species, a freak, or human aberration. Mothers routinely and needlessly warned their daughters to be careful of Nigger Bill, or Nigger Bob.

Bill lived in an abandoned "pest house" on the outskirts of Murphys. A pest house was a place to which smallpox victims were banished in the nineteenth and early twentieth centuries to live or die. They were cared for by volunteers who had had the disease and thus were immune. Bill's house was a faded, yellow-painted frame building. The windows were broken, and the wind blew through the rooms and rattled the peeling wallpaper. The roof leaked. Bill lived in one room. He boarded up the window. He nailed corrugated tin sheets to the roof over his room. There was a three-legged stove, a crude, hand-made wooden chair, a coal-oil lamp, and a mattress on the floor. Firewood was piled in empty rooms. The people in Murphys never went near the house, even before Bill moved in. They said that smallpox germs never died. The germs inhabited the walls, the floors, and the attic. They said that when the last residents left the house, their faces were like raw beefsteak. They said niggers didn't catch smallpox as easily as white folks did.

Bill never had a steady job. He cut wood, trimmed trees, raked leaves, slopped hogs, dug ditches, worked the hay fields in season. He moved outdoor privies. He collected garbage from the TB Sanitarium. If there was a dirty job to be done, it was given to Nigger Bill with an air of benevolent charity. He shot sick animals. When a horse or cow or dog took sick, the owner would send for Nigger Bill. For five dollars, Bill would shoot a horse or cow and bury it. He did his shooting with a long-barreled Colt revolver. He killed cleanly. He never shot anything twice. He walked directly up to the animal and shot it straight between the eyes. He killed calmly and without emotion. He killed all the hogs at hog killings. Killing sick animals efficiently was his only claim to self-expression. He had no opportunity to create any other kind of image for himself. He never became a provocation to white folks. He walked the back paths of humanity, threading his way like a black wraith, carefully and inoffensively through a cultural no man's land. No one ever knew his thoughts or his emotions. In the backfields, he stopped and talked with horses. One old-timer said Nigger Bill could do anything with horses. Bill did not catch the smallpox. He died of bleeding ulcers.

A persistent story had it that Bill broke with his mother for bearing him to a Negro father and creating of him a non-person. There is no verification of the story, but it seems probable. It was said they never again spoke to each other. It is possible Mary had cherished the hope that young William, "SooNOrah" educated, might one day redeem her own blighted and sordid life. For to her, as an Indian, the signs must have been propitious: A child born to her by a father who was neither Indian nor white and who appeared, mysteriously, from nowhere and in the waning months of her fertility. It is likely Mary had never before seen or heard of a Black man. It is also likely she believed that he had imparted a strange and numinous power to herself and to her son, which made her disappointment in young William and their parting the more bitter. Perhaps her determination to teach me the Miwok tongue was a frustrated transferal of maternal yearning and affection, along with the determination to leave something positive of herself behind. And perhaps my warm relationship with her was simply coincidental in its beginning, nothing more than a natural response to my gathering of acorns, which were both the staple and symbolic food of the Miwok people.

One thing, however, is certain: After Bill left her and moved to Murphys, Mary's anger and bitterness kept her in constant trouble. She made small purchases at stores in Douglas Flat and Murphys and refused to pay. "Too MUCH," she would shout. She stole a washing off a clothesline in broad daylight. It was as if she wanted to be caught. She began refusing to move out of the road for cars. If the drivers honked their horns, she threw rocks. She carried pockets full of rocks. She forced the cars to drive around her. She yelled obscenities for no apparent reason. She stopped at the parsonage in Murphys one day. The minister's wife was working in her garden. With her black, malicious grin, Mary asked the woman if "preacher like fokum. Dees way?" She raised her skirts and thrust her pelvis back and forth. The minister's wife fled in tears into the house. Later, the minister accosted Mary and gave her a stern lecture. Mary listened quietly until the minister finished. Then she leaned forward and put her hands on her hips. "BULLSHIT," she yelled, spraying him with spittle. "FOKE YOU, Charlieee." Shocked, the minister stepped back. He walked away, stumbling, and looking over his shoulder. Mary thrust her hips back and forth and gave him the finger.

But these were directed outbursts, not random and irrational manifestations of hatred. Merchants did overcharge Indians, counting on their innocence of the value of money. I know of an instance where an Indian was charged three dollars for a twenty-five cent jug of putrid wine. The washing Mary stole belonged to a woman who had hired her to do a day's work. Mary understood she was to have been paid a dollar. The woman gave her a ten-cent loaf of bread. The pious minister's son was a roadside patron of Mary. And automobile drivers could not resist tormenting her by horn honking.

There is a satisfying irony in these stories. As she grew very old, Mary became, in a real sense, the conscience of Murphys, a drunken, mean, and shambling old spectre with a memory like an elephant, who took perverse delight in revealing hypocrisy wherever she chanced onto it, whether it was to be found in a sedate gentleman strolling with his family—especially with his family—or in a gathering of the self-proclaimed "pillars of society." It reached the point where a man was afraid to appear on the streets with his wife or girl friend lest Mary spot him and shout "Hey Charlie, where you be? You no come see Mary wan year, two now." Or "Hey Charlie, SOHNA-WAHBEECH, you owe Mary one dolla!" It is true, also, that Mary began including the innocent along with the guilty; but this was done in a more subtle, even psychological way. She would walk by a man and woman, nod her head elaborately and say "How DO." But just before she passed out of the couple's hearing, she would burst into cackling laughter. One can only imagine the suspicions and angry exchange that must have taken place between the woman and the unfortunate and innocent man. "She put the Indian sign on the whole goddam town," one old-timer said.

Mary's war on Murphys climaxed, fittingly, on the Fourth of July. The Fourth of July was Murphys' favorite holiday. The trunks of the tall locust trees that lined both sides of main street were freshly whitewashed. The squared-crescent horse trough built by my grandfather was painted red, white, and blue. Iron-shuttered doors of ancient stone buildings were swung open with a loud, rusty clanging, and fireworks were sold across their old, oaken bars and counters. On the fifth of July, the doors would clang shut for another year. The Big Bridge in the center of town was draped with red, white, and blue streamers. Red, white, and blue bunting was entwined in picket fences, festooned the lower branches of the locust trees, and wrapped around the historical marker which proclaimed Joaquin Murieta, the semi-fictional bandit, to be Murphys' very own. The ceiling of the dance hall was hung with canopies of red, white, and blue streamers. Long tables set up in the brambled amphitheaters of Jungle Park were covered with red, white, and blue paper. Flags hung from windows. Murphys' Fourth of July festivities always began with a morning parade. In the afternoon, there was a picnic in Jungle Park. Women baked cakes and cookies. On the morning of the Fourth, the women got out their hand-cranked freezers and churned out a sweet-tasting ice cream. The day ended with a dance.

On this Fourth of July, as always, the parade gathered in a field east of Murphys by the Big Pine. The Big Pine stood at the forks of roads that led south to Angels Camp and east to the Adams Ranch. It was the largest blue-needled Digger or bull pine in Calaveras County. It might well have been the largest of its kind in California. It was whitewashed up to its lower branches, which were thicker than the trunks of ordinary trees. The Big Pine was both a landmark and a symbol. In the 1850s, it had been a hangman's tree. A miner recorded that when he first entered Murphys in 1852, two men were swinging from its lower limbs. Distance was measured by the Big Pine. It was said to stand exactly one mile from the center of

Murphys. On pleasant evenings, people took walks out to the Big Pine and back. Boys raced their cars out to the Big Pine.

On this day, as always, the parade formed in the field and snaked ritualistically around the Big Pine to take its shape, like a rope fed through a pulley. First came the "Indians," white men and women decked out in feathers. Some of the younger men wore breechclouts. The one or two Miwoks who marched in the parade were drunk. They staggered along, grinning foolishly. They wore blue jeans and blue denim shirts. Next were a half-dozen old-timers leading burros. They wore red shirts and bib-overalls. The burros bore wooden pack-saddles to which were lashed picks, shovels, mining pans, and canvas tarps. The red-shirted Miners Band followed. Each band member wore a miner's cap affixed with a lighted and flickering carbide lamp. Light smoke from the lamps wreathed and swirled to the blasting of the music. Horsemen followed the band. The horses were an eclectic bunch, plodding along in various shapes, sizes, colors, and states of decrepitude. Their riders wore woolly and leather chaps, high-heeled boots, and sombreros and looked very self-conscious. Sudden blasts of band music made the horses nervous, and they left great yellow piles of dung in the road. Last came the vintage cars, the Pierce Arrows, Durants, Paiges, Veelies, Jewetts, Oaklands, Overlands, and Willys Knights. The cars were painted bright colors, and their brass parts gleamed with a high polish. The drivers steered their cars carefully around the piles of dung.

Just as the last car, a long and shiny black Jewett touring car with a canvas top, circled the Big Pine, Mary came clip-clopping down the Adams Ranch Road in a two wheeled cart drawn by a very old, sway-backed white horse and joined the parade directly behind the Jewett. She had been watching the parade take shape from the brow of a low hill, just off the road. The horse and cart belonged to her squaw-man. Mary wore a clean gray blouse and long black skirt and high buttoned black boots. On her head was a stiff-brimmed, black-lacquered straw hat. Affixed to the crown of the black hat was a smaller, red-lacquered straw hat. Perched on top of the red hat and bristling with long, head-beaded hatpins that held it in place was a large, dung-stippled bird's nest. An artificial flower rose from the birds' nest on its wire stem. The flower was painted in the orange and black colors and design of the Tiger Lily. It bobbed back and forth to the moving cart.

As the parade crawled through Murphys, Mary's progress at its tail was measured in bursts of laughter at her hat and by crude shouts. "Hey Mary, where you gittum heap big hat?" "Where's the birdie?" Mary did not respond. She did not once look to left or right. Her old white horse stumbled along. His eyes were closed. He slept when the parade paused. Often he would stumble to a halt, his head drooping. Mary shook the reins gently against the sagging old back. He would wake with a start and stagger on. Mary held close to the gleaming black Jewett whose driver was furious. He had spent days waxing and polishing his car. Now every one looked at Mary's hat and laughed. Several times he stopped and motioned angrily for her to pass. Mary stared at him impassively. She had taken for her province that day the last place in the parade. The procession moved on. Mary's artificial Tiger Lily bobbled back and forth from its bird's nest. Once the Jewett stopped and the horse, asleep, bumped his head against the canvas back and left a wide, foam-flecked saliva stain. The driver cursed and drove on. The horse went back to sleep. Mary rattled the reins. "Show 'im that hat, Mary," some one shouted. "That'll wake 'im up." "Hold his head up, Mary, or his teeth'll fall out." Mary endured the taunts stoically. She made no reply. She held her head up and gazed ahead. When the last of the parade turned left between Bob's Inn and the Sperry Hotel for Jungle Park, Mary rode straight on. The liberated Jewett driver shook his fist. The crowd on the hotel balcony shouted at her as she plodded past. Their shouts were brutish and racial: "Where you gittem' heap big birdshit hat, Mary? You eatum' up baby birds?" Mary did not look up. She turned her old horse north toward Rocky Hill where a half-dozen Indians were camped.

That afternoon at the picnic in Jungle Park, people laughed and talked about Mary. Each had his or her own theory of what had cohered in her mind, of why she entered the parade uninvited and wore that outlandish hat: It was to make the parade look ridiculous. She was mocking the town by making fun of the parade. She was angry because of the phony Indians. The Jewett owner was certain it was because Mary hated cars. It was his bad luck to ride tandem with her. He should have backed up, he said, and run over her. I have always had my own opinion, and I hold to it. I think Mary simply wanted to belong, to be, finally, and late in her life, a part of something. Indians are communal. But there were too few Indians left at that time for any kind of focused communal activity. I believe she thought her hat a creation of beauty, that the bird's nest was intended as a symbol which, along with the artificial Tiger Lily, blended the natural world with the mechanical world of the white man, a symbolic drawing together in an even and flowing movement. What better way than a parade, to her a moving ceremony, of revealing her mind, of innocently and honestly exposing the raw material of the human spirit. It was the Indian way. She was sober. She was carefully and neatly dressed. She did not respond or even react to taunts. She put herself bravely on display. I believe she joined the parade as a peace offering. Murphys thought her ridiculous, a chimerical manifestation, and disgraced her with its laughter.

The Murphys dance hall is reputedly one of the oldest of its kind in California. It is a long, squat wooden structure that

thrusts out over a limestoned gulch. It rests on limestone out-
croppings on one side and tall timbers on the other. The space
below the dance hall measures fifteen feet from ground to floor
bottom. Once a noisy little brook ran catercornered under the
hall and emptied into Murphys Creek. An outdoor-type privy,
entered from inside the hall, was located directly over the brook.
It was said to be the only toilet in Murphys with a natural
flushing action. There was a short front porch to the dance hall
with steps at either end. A stout railing closed it in. Two heavy
oak doors swung open onto the porch. Inside, directly in front
of the doors and about six feet forward, was a wooden partition which shut out the view of the dancers from the open
door. To the left of the doors, in the corner of the hall, was a
huge, cast-iron stove. Chunks of oak and pine wood were
stacked against the wall. The stove stood inside a triangle formed
of two wooden benches that ran at an angle from near the
doors to the left wall. Indians were permitted to stand inside
the triangle. They were not permitted to dance, nor could they
even venture onto the floor. Everywhere they saw and heard
the signs and sounds of their exclusion. Wooden benches lined
both sides of the hall, and the front of the three-foot high stage
at the far end where the musicians sat.

At 11:00 P.M., the evening of the day Mary drove her cart in
the parade, the dance floor was crowded. Music blared from a
seven piece orchestra. Under the canopied red, white, and blue
streamers, the dancers bounced to *The Varsity Drag*. Four hours
later, at 3:00 A.M., the band would play *Good Night Ladies*, and
the streamers would be ceremonially pulled down. The benches
along the walls were packed. The odor of raviolis and macaroni
drifted up the stairs from the kitchen, which was located under
the back of the stage. At midnight everyone would cue up and
shuffle down the stairway to supper served on long, paper-
covered tables.

Suddenly the dancers near the door stopped dancing and began to crowd back upon the center of the hall. A loud buzz went up and settled quickly to a murmur. The music stopped, and the musicians stood up to see what the commotion was. Now, no one was dancing. The crowd began pushing back upon itself, toward the walls and the stage, forming a wide circle. The spectators stood on the benches to look over the crowd. Mary had somehow got by the door keeper, moved around the partition and was staggering, dead-drunk, toward the center of the hall. The crowd parted before her like an unraveling hemstitch. Mary stood in the center of a wide circle. Her vomit-encrusted mouth sagged loosely open in a perpetual smile. She drooled. She had been drinking red wine. The front to of her blouse was a carapace of dried, red vomit. The hat was gone. Her hair hung to her shoulders. Heavy strands lay wet with perspiration against her face. Bits of dry grass and leaves clung to her skirts. Almost uniformly, the faces in the crowd were frozen in expressions of horror and revulsion.

Mary stood swaying and looking around at the thickly-packed crowd. She pointed to a man squirming backward into the wall of flesh. "Hey Charlie," she yelled. "Where you go? You no come see Mary wan week, now, maybeso 'tree." The man's dancing partner turned away and pushed through the crowd toward the door. The man followed. Now Mary began stabbing her finger seemingly at random into the crowd, but wherever she pointed, it was said, a man was seen to be burrowing guiltily into the mass of humanity, figuratively impaled on Mary's pointing finger. "Hey Charlie, you got 'nother WOOMAHN? Mary no goot FOKUM no moah? No moah goot, barn, grass?" The silence, I am told, was horrible, palpable. It was difficult to tell if the silent fascination was with Mary, or the objects of her pointing finger.

Mary now spotted the people standing on the benches. Al-

FIG 18. Old Lucy, a mute with mutilated legs.
Killed by white boys—Murphys. Courtesy
Bill Harper.

most directly in front of her stood a half dozen teen-age boys
whose mothers had mounted the benches beside them. Mary's
accusing finger traced the air slowly and maliciously upward,
riveting mothers and sons to their perch. "Gottam poys no
GOOT," she shouted. "Like FOKUM, no like PAY. Maybeso
you MAMA's pay." She pointed to one of the women. "YOU
pay," she demanded loudly. The woman scrambled down from
the bench, yanking her son along. Mary laughed. Pointing to
each of the mothers, she began to stamp her feet and clap her
hands and chant, "YOU pay? YOU pay? YOU pay?" Mothers

and sons were struggling down from the benches, pushing at the people jammed up against them. They fought their way through the crowd toward the door.

Except for Mary's drunken shouts and laughter, the silence held. Then, on that Fourth of July night, the orchestra suddenly struck up *The Star Spangled Banner*. Mary lurched about and faced the stage, and as the crowd gasped, she raised her skirts and began humping lewdly to the music. By the time the piece had progressed raggedly to "the rockets red glare," Mary's humps and thrust and bumps and grinds were so well coordinated with the lyrics—one hump for "the," two for "rockets," one for "red," and three wicked thrusts for "glare"—the orchestra fizzled and bubbled out as if it had been dunked in water. In the musical pause that endured, Mary again staggered about her circle, peering into the crowd. She spotted a tall, gray-haired man struggling towards the door. His wife followed, stony-faced. Mary stumbled along the edge of the crowd, following. "Hey Charlie, you WOOMAHN bettah fokum Mary? WOOMANH go dees way?" She thrust her hips forward in a shockingly obscene manner. The woman pushed ahead of her husband and ran out the door.

Someone had sent for the constable. The Constable was a little old man. He was believed to be in his late eighties. His hair was white and his dark, beady eyes were barely separated by a long, hooked and red nose. He suffered from a form of ataxia. When he walked, his shoulders and arms swung backward and forward and his legs kicked out and looped in circular steps. Under stress, he would sometimes walk in place, as though on a treadmill. His legs would flair out uncontrollably. On occasion, he would slip into reverse and go flailing crazily backward until he bumped into something and stopped. The story goes that the Constable was asleep behind his desk when he was summoned by his deputy. A star was pinned to his shirt.

He awakened, confused from sleep and doubtless also from age. He stumbled around his tiny office. He took his pistol from his desk drawer, then put it back. He absent-mindedly pinned on another star. Before he left his office, he had fumbled on a third star. At his age and in his physical condition, he owed his constabulary solely to a youthful service as shotgun messenger for Wells Fargo. He was a relic with a badge; in this instance three of them.

The Constable entered the hall, the three stars gleaming from his shirt, a veritable galaxy of law and order. The crowd opened a path to Mary's circle. The Constable walked slowly. His legs had begun to twitch. Convulsions fluttered up and down his trousers. He jerked spasmodically as he fought for control. Mary saw the crowd open. She stared as the Constable walked slowly into her circle, his legs flicking out at intervals. They stood facing each other, the old, vomit-caked and drooling Indian woman, her mouth agape, and the twitching, spasmodic little constable, both wretched parodies of another time, now the sole center of attention in a wide, human circle of silence.

The Constable tried to set himself, to put more weight on his legs to hold them in place.

"Mary," he said. "You GO."

"SOHNAWAHBEECH." Mary exclaimed, pointing to the three stars. "HE BEEG MAHN."

The constable looked down. For the first time, he was aware of the three stars. He jerked spasmodically. His legs began to flail, and he commenced to walk in place. His feet slapped against the floor.

"Mary," he shouted. "You GO, NOW." Mary stared at the thrashing legs, her mouth hanging open. Suddenly she laughed.

"You like DANCE Mary, Charlie?" She pulled up her skirts and began humping and thrusting to the Constable's thrashing legs. "He-YA, He-YA, He-YA," she chanted.

"NO," The Constable yelled. "You GO. Git!"

"FOKE YOU Charlieee," Mary sang. "He-YA, he-YA, he-YA." She kept humping and thrusting and chanting while the Constable's legs flailed and jerked. The crowd and the musicians seemed immobilized while Mary and The Constable stood humping and jerking in a grotesque *danse macabre*.

Yelling for Mary to "Go," The Constable slipped into reverse. He went thrashing and yelling backward with the stunned crowd pushing away before him until he was brought up against the wooden partition before the door. He stood pressed against the partition. His feet banged and thumped against the wall until he slid slowly to a sitting position where his heels drummed an elegiac tattoo against the floor. Mary broke the silence and the immobility.

"LOOOOOK!" she sang. "SOHNAWAHBEECH! Leg go CRAAA-ZEE!"

Now two men ran to the Constable and carried him, still kicking, outside. The orchestra grabbed up its instruments and blasted out *Good Night Ladies*. Mary whirled and humped and thrust to the music while the crowd broke for the door, leaving her humping and hooting with laughter inside a wide crescent of flowing humanity. The musicians left by the stage door which opened onto an alley. In a few moments, Mary stood alone under a canopy of red, white, and blue streamers.

Early that morning the old horse and cart was seen and heard clopping through Murphys. Mary had passed out and slid from the seat to the floorboards, where she lay crumpled. One arm flung out the back between the creaking wooden-spoked wheels. The horse would plod a few yards, then stop and sleep. It would awaken with a feeble snort and slowly stumble on. In this manner, the horse and cart progressed through Murphys and brought up, finally, before the squaw-man's cabin in Douglas Flat.

Two days later Mary appeared in Murphys, outwardly the soul of aboriginal contrition. She wore a clean gray blouse and long black skirt. Her high-buttoned shoes were polished. Her braids encircled her head and were held in place by hatpins. She walked slowly up and down main street. She was elaborately polite to everyone she met. "How DO, mees? How DO, meester?" She made polite little bows. She did not laugh. She did not call anyone "Charlie." She savored the town's humiliation. In the afternoon, she went up to the "Indian Camp" and got drunk. Late that night, staggering along an isolated stretch of road midway between Murphys and Douglas Flat, just under the crest of a hill, she was struck down by a car and badly injured. It was said that it was not a hit-and-run accident, but I have not been able to learn the name of the car's driver. It was said that the coroner was summoned to pick her up, which led to the first story that she had been killed. I am told she lay in the hospital cursing the *too-KOO-loo-loo* until she was released. She did not come to Murphys again. She died a few months later. The collective sigh of relief from the male "pillars of Murphys' society," the good 'ol "Charlies," now secure in their ankle-deep clay and able to devote all their concerns to Amos 'n' Andy, must have been nearly audible. I am certain it never occurred to them that Mary probably had tasted her mortal being and had courted her death; she wanted the white man to be responsible for it.

I am unable to this day to sort out my thoughts and feelings about Mary to my own satisfaction. I saw her only through a child's eyes, and though I have tried to tell her story true, and with the historian's objectivity, I have doubtless idealized her as I probably did Aaron. I don't know why she tried so hard to teach me the Miwok language. Perhaps as with Walker and Mike Marshal, she was impelled to pass on something of herself, of her people, if only the language. Indian children were learning English. It is possible I was the only vessel at hand for the transport of at least the language part of her culture. Yet it was more than just that. She was touched by me as I was touched by her. I know that many of her visits to Murphys were solely to teach me the language, to be with me. Once she waited all afternoon for me to return from a visit, sitting out on our oak root, humming softly to herself. Later, she walked home in the dark. Mary was able to lovingly separate the child from the society that had used her so brutally. I know of no instance when a white woman so attended any Indian child, or attended one at all, for that matter. When Mary died, I sensed that something vital had passed forever from my life, something I could not quite comprehend. I went out to our oak root as much in dismay as in sorrow. I thought of her tracks in the snow and of how they had filled and disappeared as she had now disappeared under a filling of earth. I was brought face to face with the restless and endless recomposition of nature. Perhaps she had intended that I learn that, too; that immortality lies in what one passes on in the warmth and memories of human relationships, not just in the volatility of the external world. I am wondering if that is why I write this now. I sat on our root and said all the Indian words and phrases she had taught me. I was surprised that I actually spoke her language. But somehow I knew that though she was gone, her vital and humane center had held against the way she had been used, the cruelties she had suffered, and that she had taken it safely with her to her grave in the pines alongside Aaron. For a long time, though, my wounds from her loss stayed fresh and painful.

FIVE

Andy

Andy was a "good Indian." All the white folks said so. He wore a perpetual smile, not the smile of imbecility or of obsequy, but one that bespoke a genuinely sunny nature. Even the blackened stumps of his teeth did not diminish his smile. Men saw in his opalescent eyes the intelligent appraisal of one who acted upon his own beliefs and decisions, an engaged personality who was neither arrogant nor servile. He approached Indian and white on an equal and friendly basis. He was anomalous among his people who were either sullen and angry or timid and compliant. They lived without expectations and in brutal subjection to their meaningless lives. Suicide was endemic among the California Miwok.

During the 1920s and early 1930s, Andy lived in an abandoned miner's cabin midway between Murphys and Sheep Ranch. The cabin was a board and batten structure built stoutly on a rock foundation. It stood in a small yellow pine grove near a willow-sheathed stream. Trout swam in the deeper pools and under tiny waterfalls. The grove was partly closed in by red manzanita and chaparral. The ground was carpeted with brown pine needles. There was a large, single-paned window by the cabin door, a gift from an Italian merchant who kept a store in Sheep Ranch. The Merchant, a widower, was Andy's closest friend. He was also a craftsman of sorts. He helped Andy to enlarge the old window and frame the new one in. The window faced East, the sacred direction for all Indians, the direction from which *hiema* (the sun) appeared. The Merchant was interested in the Indians' belief in the sun. He thought it lacked the artificiality of Christianity. The Indians' worship was of Nature, not of sacred objects or relics. They saw the Earth as in a constant state of recomposition and restoration that was perceivable in the volatility of the seasons, in fires begun by lightening, rainstorms that altered watercourses, the colors of the fall, the dry and wet seasons. Nature was restless and dissatisfied, and in a constant state of change and renewal. It demanded placatory ceremonies. Each morning Andy stood before his window and made his devotions to the rising sun. He watched the shafts of pine-filtered light slide across the floor. He marveled at the crystalline particles of dusty colors that moved restlessly in the prismatic beams.

During the winter months, Andy ran a trapline. Trapping to him was both a business and a precise science. He set out close to one hundred and fifty traps. His trapline was twenty miles or more long. It meandered along ridge crests, near clumps of rocks, around the edges of clearings and along abandoned trails and wagon roads. He wrapped tinfoil around trap pans and set them in running water. Curious raccoons were irresistibly drawn to the deadly glitter. He studied signs. Because of their color or brightness, white rocks often bore deposits of ordure that plainly marked out a territory. Andy had become something of an expert on scatology: coyote scat contained hair; fox and coon droppings were stippled with red manzanita berries.

He made his sets according to the different kinds of scat and their disposition. He could identify spoor at a glance: coyote tracks described a straight line; they did not splay out like those of a dog. Coon tracks were like baby feet. The prints of foxes were catlike without claws, those of a skunk formed a sharper and clawed outline and moved erratically in scurrying patterns. Andy admired the beauty of Nature. He once told his friend, the Merchant, that the prettiest sight he had ever seen was a prime, black and white striped skunk hurrying across a carpet of brown pine needles with a brisk wind ruffling its fur. It was said he could touch the impress of a deer bed in leaves or pine needles with his finger tips and tell almost exactly when the deer had left its bed.

Andy tended his trapline every other day. On the days between, he skinned and stretched the previous day's catch on racks to dry. He shipped his furs in bundles to Roger's Fur House in Denver, Colorado. On good days he might take two coyotes, two coons, two or three foxes, and several skunks. At that time, fur prices were listed in catalogs. A coyote fur brought five dollars, a coon three, foxes a dollar to a dollar and a quarter, skunks sixty-five to seventy-five cents. On such a day, Andy told the Merchant, he would make twenty dollars or more. Seven or eight dollars was a poor day. These were rare. The going wage for a skilled worker at that time was five dollars a day, eighteen hundred a year. Andy earned that much in the four months of the trapping season. He bought a large iron stove with an oven on credit. He paid for it in cash with his first month's catch. When the season ended in March, Andy took up his traps. He hung them neatly in groups on the outside walls of the cabin according to make and size numbers.

Spring was a time of renewal, of restoration, a time for being Indian, time to savor Nature at her most benevolent and bountiful, to hold all senses open and receptive. Andy told his friend the Merchant that he spent days just walking about the countryside. He flung himself upon Nature. He rolled in the new grass that rippled before the wind, and he smelled the warm fecundity of the damp earth. He watched clouds of spermatozoic dust blow from pine candles and shower onto the earth. He was seized with spasms of joy during which he thanked the Spirits for the providence and beauty of the land, and he thanked the animals who gave him their furs. The air was filled with birdsong. Sap rose in the trees. Oaks leafed out in pale greens. There was the sweet smell of flowering chaparral. The earth was a rainbow of colors, meadows brilliant with yellow mustard and purple lupine; mauve forget-me-nots and pink Indian paintbrush; violet, yellow-nosed Johnny-jump-ups; clusters of cerise, blue, pink and white phlox; orange tiger lilies with their distinctive black markings; and higher up, in little clumps deep in the pines, were the rare red and tuberous snow plants. Water ran swift and clear in tessellated stream beds. Everywhere, the earth throbbed with life. It was a time to be one with Nature. It was a time to be Indian.

To the Indian mind, nothing is accidental in Nature. Their universe, emanating from the Four Directions, moves with intent and meaning. The ephemeral prodigality of spring puts one of a mind and temperament to endure a hot and dry summer; the kaleidoscopic colors of fall, along with its vagrant and fitful weather rhythms, lures one on into a possibly harsh winter. Nature repeats itself, but not precisely. It rewards and punishes. In summer, the field and meadow grasses of the Sierra foothills turn yellowish white. Streams shrink to a trickle. Fish are trapped in shallow pools. The sun is brassy in color. Andy cut wood during the summer. He cut to order. In 1930, he bought a secondhand, two-seated Model A Ford that had been converted into a truck. He hauled the cut wood to the clearing near his cabin and stacked it to dry in the sun. He stacked it according to orders taken, in tiers and cords. He made his deliveries between the first and tenth of October. I do not know what he was paid for his wood.

Fall was the time of preparation for the winter trapline. Early in the spring, Andy had cut cedar branches and piled them near his cabin to dry. Now he cut a long pole and thrust it through the crotches of two trees some ten or twelve feet apart. He hung his traps in groups along the pole. He piled the dry cedar branches under the traps and set them afire. He heaped the cedar on heavily. A dense cloud of smoke curled around the traps. Cedar smoke kills human scent. He hung two pairs of gloves on the pole. He would not touch the traps again without the gloves. From mid October to November fifteenth, the opening of the trapping season, Andy scouted a new trapline. He studied the signs and made mental notes. He moved evenly with the seasons. There was time, now, to visit more often with his friend, the Merchant. The evenings were sharp and brisk. Fall gave the earth a new definition. Everywhere there was color: the red-gold of oaks, the yellow of willow, and higher, the shimmering gold of aspen; even the sere grasses held a subdued glow, and the green bracken along stream banks was tinged with color. Andy made all his purchases from the Merchant's store. He carried a *chomuck* sack and recited his needs. The Merchant always slipped extra items into Andy's sack: a can of tuna, a sack of Bull Durham, an extra tin of coffee, a loaf of bread, a can of peaches. He was careful to avoid offense by giving too much. Andy never acknowledged the extras. That was not the Indian way. He responded in kind. He would drive up with a tier of wood and stack it in the Merchant's shed. He would fetch a haunch of deer and hang it in the cellar. The two men had an understanding. They sat around the Merchant's store of fall evenings. The Merchant wrapped and addressed Andy's fur bundles for shipping. He cashed checks. He taught Andy rudimentary reading and writing. He taught him how to make lists of his needs. Andy learned quickly. He was always pleased with his progress. The Merchant said that within a year Andy had nearly the equivalent of a fourth or a fifth grade education. In turn, the Merchant learned the rudiments of the Penutian tongue.

One very cold, early December night, Andy and the Merchant sat talking by the store's big stove. They were discussing the prime quality of furs that winter. It was at that time a big black cat walked past the stove and looked up at Andy. Andy laughed. "Now there's a prime pelt," he said, "and I didn't even have to trap him." He reached down and picked the cat up. He stroked the heavy fur. The cat settled in his lap. It purred loudly. Its big yellow eyes closed. It flexed its claws.

"That there's Nigger," the Merchant said. "He just moved in a couple of weeks ago, and he's already got my two cats knocked up."

Andy laughed. "Nigger," he said softly. "Nigger." He shook his head. "Know what I'd call him if he was mine?"

"What?"

"Whiteman. I'd call him Whiteman." They laughed. Andy stroked the cat. He held it all evening.

A month later Andy brought the Merchant a venison roast and a half-dozen large steaks. Andy had venison the year round. He had quail. He hunted from need as his people had hunted from the Dream Time. The white man had imposed the artificial hunting seasons. Andy obeyed the laws of Nature. The white man's laws concurred with Nature only during the trapping season when furs were prime. That was the one time the white man observed Nature's law. Now the Merchant filled Andy's *chomuck* according to the Indian's scrawled list. He stuffed in the usual extra. He did not thank Andy for the venison roast and steaks. Thanks, he had learned, was meaningless to Indians.

The meaning of something was perceived through reciprocity, not empty words. As Andy prepared to leave, the Merchant asked him to wait a minute. He reached under the counter and came up with a squirming little black ball of fur. "Here's Whiteman," he said, smiling.

Years later, the Merchant told me of Andy's boyish delight with the kitten. He stroked its tiny head with a forefinger. He laughed and shook his head. He was surprised by the blue eyes. The Merchant told him that all kittens had blue eyes. They turned yellow later. Andy fed the kitten warm, condensed milk. As it grew, he fed it venison and sometimes fish he seined from the stream. When he was two years old, Whiteman was an unusually large cat. His black fur was thick and sleek. His yellow eyes blazed. Except for the days when Andy walked his trapline, he and Whiteman were inseparable. When Andy went about his outside chores, the big cat trotted behind. When he stood, Whiteman twisted in and out between his legs. Often Andy reached down and stroked the cat, which arched its back sharply against his hand. As Andy worked at dressing his furs, Whiteman lay purring loudly and watching through half closed eyes. He had taken as his province a place under the eaves inside the cabin. He ascended his lofty perch by an angled catwalk Andy made for him. At night, when Andy worked by lantern light on the day's catch, Whiteman lay in his nest, invisible in the dark recesses of the eaves save for the yellow blaze of his eyes.

Andy had saved four-hundred dollars. He kept twenty, twenty dollar bills folded neatly in a Prince Albert tobacco can. The can was hidden in a niche he had hollowed out in the top of the cabin's center cross-beam. It could not be seen from the floor. He intended to add another room to his cabin, one with a tramped earth floor and a mud and rock fireplace. He would build a shed farther out with cross-stringers on which to hang his furs. He told the Merchant where the money was in the event that something happened to him. He was again anomalous among his people for his planning, for not perceiving the meaning of his life through its neglect.

It was in January of '33, the Merchant told me, that Andy went to Murphys and met Bessie. The Merchant said that nothing more disastrous could have happened to a man as innocent as Andy. Bessie was a "mean squaw." She lived with any man who would keep her, Indian or white. Three times, different men had had her arrested for using a knife on them. Bessie claimed self-defense. The men had beaten her. She preferred men who treated her badly. Between men, she lived in a tiny and filthy cabin on a hill near an abandoned mine. She whored openly. Six young white men admitted to taking turns with her in her cabin. She smelt of fish and sweat, they said. As each finished with her she yelled, "fifty cents!" Her head was large, her hair thick and greasy. Her black eyes were "mean." She never smiled. She was heavy and big breasted. She wore blouses that were too small. The cloth pulled apart between buttons through which ellipses of brown flesh protruded. Andy fell in love with her. He was completely without guile, and he could only respond helplessly to what he saw and felt. He paid no attention to the warnings of friends, both Indian and white. He told the Merchant he was taking a woman. When the Merchant learned that the woman was Bessie, he quietly suggested that Andy not hurry such an important move, that he might want to get better acquainted with the woman. He would not affront his friend with a direct warning. Andy laughed. He was happy. The next day he brought Bessie to his cabin. It was early January. "I knew then," the Merchant said, "that the serpent was in the garden."

A little over a week after he had brought Bessie to his cabin, Andy appeared at the Merchant's store. He did not carry his *chomuck*. He brought no meat. His eyes were dark pits of fear and bewilderment. Haltingly, he described what had to have been for one of his innocence, a week of pure hell. Bessie had insisted on bringing four or five bottles of whiskey to the cabin. She was drunk, Andy said, from morning to night. (Again, Andy was anomalous among his people: he did not drink.) Bessie yelled and cursed and broke things. She ran Whiteman out of the cabin. The cat was terrified. Black cats were bad luck, she said. They were evil spirits. Once she kicked Whiteman hard in the hip. The cat had squalled and run limping into the woods. He had not come back. Andy told Bessie about the four-hundred dollars in the crossbeam. He told her of his plans for it. When he came in from his trapline early that afternoon, Bessie was gone. There was a chair positioned under the center cross-beam. The Prince Albert can lay on the floor. Andy was going to Murphys. Maybe, he told the Merchant, he could change her mind. Maybe he could help her.

The Merchant spoke quietly and carefully. Was it worth it? Wouldn't she just do it again? There was the theft of the four-hundred dollars. People can change, Andy said. Maybe he could help her stop drinking. And since she was his woman, the money was hers, too. It was not a theft. The Merchant said no more. He wished his friend luck.

Two weeks later the Merchant learned what had happened. During that time, he had heard nothing from Andy. He assumed that he had talked Bessie into coming back to the cabin. He was under no illusions that Andy had changed her. Bessie was a product of brutality. She responded in kind. If Andy had been rejected, he was shamed; he would want to be alone. The Merchant had resisted the impulse to go to the cabin. Now a friend from Murphys told him the story:

Bessie had taken up with a squaw-man called Big Red. Big Red was a bully, notorious for his brutality to Indian women and to Indian men who resented him. He was tall and muscular. His hair was close-cropped and light red. His eyes were small and dull, his nose was large and humped. He claimed Sioux ancestry. He worked sometimes as a logger. Mostly, he lived off the labor of Indian women, often as a pimp. Bessie had obviously brought him Andy's four-hundred dollars. The two had been drinking steadily in the Murphy's Hotel bar the day Bessie left Andy's cabin, and paying for their drinks from a roll of twenty dollar bills. It was midafternoon when Andy walked into the bar. He had tried to talk to Bessie. She was drunk. She screamed and spat on him. She scratched at his face. It was while Andy tried to hold her off, to calm her, that Big Red attacked him. The Merchant's friend had not seen what had happened, but he saw Andy immediately afterward. Andy's nose, he said, was smashed. His mouth and lips were crushed. His face was a mask of blood. His left eye was badly damaged, a pool of blood from which a clear matter flowed. The friend feared that Andy had been blinded in the eye. As Andy lay unconscious on the floor, Big Red kicked him viciously in the ribs before some men dragged him away. When Andy regained consciousness, he coughed blood. He could not talk. He could barely stand. His eye had apparently been cut by a ring Big Red was wearing. Andy would not let the men take him to a doctor in Angels Camp. He was helped into his car. Bessie stood in the hotel doorway hooting and laughing at him.

"I felt sick," the Merchant told me. He knew that even if Andy had survived so brutal a beating, now none of the circumstances of life gave him reason or cause to live. With the "sick feeling" riding in his stomach, the Merchant drove to Andy's cabin. As he drove, he conjured the image of a life purified by the idyllic innocence of living as one with Nature and by Nature's laws, of one who had never conceived of the violence that underlies all principles, one who could live happily on Nature's terms, but disastrously on those of so-called civilization.

Even above the clatter of his car, the Merchant heard Whiteman squalling as he drove into the clearing, heard and saw the big black cat leaping frantically against Andy's sun window. He cut the motor and ran to the window. Straining to see against reflected sunlight and past the leaping and squalling cat, the Merchant saw Andy lying on the floor and near his out-flung arm, the revolver. He tried the door. It was locked. Inside, Whiteman squalled and scratched and clawed against the door jamb. The Merchant, a big and strong man, kicked the door open. Whiteman burst out with a primal screech and ran squalling into the woods and on into legend.

The odor pouring through the open door was unbearable. The Merchant pulled a bandanna over his nose and mouth and tied it behind his head. He went inside. What he saw, he told me, he would remember to his dying day. The starving cat had eaten Andy's nose and most of his left cheek. It had eaten the damaged eye and licked the empty socket clean. It had cleaned out the hole where the bullet had passed out the top of Andy's head and had eaten away much of the back of his neck. There were ants swarming over Andy's face. Three dead rats lay nearby. Whiteman had torn them to pieces. The Merchant saw a piece of paper and a pencil on the table. He grabbed the paper and rushed outside. It was a note addressed to him:

> My fren, traps al sprun,
> all thins yers. Try find
> whiteman
> Andy

"I was crying for the loss of my friend and dry-heaving from the smell of his death," the Merchant said. When he shot himself, Andy had not known Whiteman was in the cabin, cowering out of sight in his lofty perch in the eaves. The Merchant theorized that Andy, blinded in one eye and confused from the beating had called the cat, which had not responded from fear of the woman, whose odor doubtless still lay heavy in the cabin. It was Andy's custom to leave the door ajar for Whiteman. The cat had returned to the cabin while Andy was in Murphys.

The Merchant foundered in his soul when he envisioned the hours leading to his friends suicide: the agonizing drive from Murphys over the twisting and hilly road to his cabin; the smashed and bleeding face; the frothy bubble of blood from internal injuries; the throbbing eye with the clear fluid of his vision seeping from it; the resolve to end his life. The Merchant conjured a picture that was more than heroic: it was epical. The perhaps fatally injured man had called upon incredible reserves of strength and will to struggle over his twenty-mile trapline to spring the traps so that caught animals might not suffer.

Years had not dimmed the Merchant's bitterness and anger. "If I had met Big Red at that moment, I'd have killed him," he said. "I know I would have." He shook his head. "White people have treated these Indians like trash. How many white men," he asked rhetorically, "in Andy's condition and in his state of mind, would have thought of suffering trapped animals? None!"

The Merchant drove away from the cabin intending to call the coroner. "But I got to thinking," he said. "The coroner would just scoop him up and bury him in the white man's cemetery under a pauper's slab. Andy wasn't a pauper. And a burial like that would not be right. It would not be fitting for a man of Andy's nobility and humanity." The Merchant decided to drive north to West Point where Andy had relatives and friends. He would consult with them.

At West Point he found Andy's cousin, Potter. The two went to the "Indian Camp." Within the hour, the word of Andy's

death had got out, and his friend's and relatives came to Potter's
house. It was freezing cold. Potter had a fire going in his cast
iron strove. The sides of the stove glowed cherry-red. The Merchant told them of Andy's death, of the woman, Bessie, and of
Big Red. He told them how Whiteman had eaten part of Andy's
face and how the big black cat had run howling into the woods
and had not been seen again. The Indians sat around the stove.
They drank coffee. Each spoke in turn. The Merchant, they
agreed, had done the right thing by coming to them. He was
Andy's friend. They would come to Sheep Ranch that night
and make a ceremony at Andy's cabin. They would neither
touch Andy nor look upon him. They would burn the cabin
and pray and make offerings as his spirit ascended with the fire
and smoke. The Merchant asked if he might take the window
he had given Andy as a symbol of their friendship. He would
place it in the eastern wall of his store and when the sun came
up, he would look for Andy's face in it. It was agreed that he
should have the window. The Merchant went back to Sheep
Ranch and picked up some tools. He drove to Andy's cabin.
He tied the bandanna over his nose and removed the window.
Then he nailed boards over the opening after making certain
that Whiteman had not returned. He tried not to look at Andy.

Just after dusk the Indians drove up to the Merchant's store
in an old dodge truck. There were three men in front and
seven crouched in the back. They were wrapped in blankets.
The Merchant thought of the old nursery rhyme: *Ten Little
Indians.* "Ten little, nine little, eight little Indians," he said to
himself, "One little Indian boy." Andy wasn't much more than
a boy, a *naña-ti,* he thought, and now they would burn him and
consign his spirit to the Happy Place. "No little Indian boy."
The Merchant spoke quietly to the Indians. Their voices were
muffled in their blankets. The temperature had dropped to six
above. The moon was full and coldly white. The Merchant put

a gallon can of gasoline in his car and drove off. The Indians followed. The moon kept pace with the cars, slipping behind ridges and gliding between trees. They drove to the edge of Andy's clearing and parked the cars. The moonlight washed through the pines. "*Walli keleli* [the Earth's white]," Potter said. "*Hu,*" the Merchant answered. (yes.)

The Merchant carried the gasoline into the cabin. He sloshed it over Andy, over the floor and walls. When he came out, the Indians had formed a crescent, with Potter at its center. Now Potter came forward. He carried a large, pitch pine knot. He spoke softly to himself. The Merchant made out some of the words, *wuke, hakisu, holi,* fire, smoke, ashes. Potter lighted the knot and tossed it through the cabin door. The cabin exploded into flames. Deep, sepulchral sounds of collective grief swelled from the Indians. There was no keening. The moans settled into a soft, lugubrious chant. They did not dance. They swayed back and forth in place as they tossed offerings into the fire: tiny bundles, tobacco, beads, some coins. The scene was surreal: the swaying and chanting Indians, that ghastly moonlight, the burning cabin and beyond, the dark shapes of trees. The Merchant's feeling was one of unreality. He was witnessing a Stone Age ceremony. He could not mentally associate the ritual with his once happy friend, Andy. When the cabin collapsed into the flames, the moans went up again. Then the Indians fell silent. Potter said something the Merchant did not understand. The Indians walked in a line to the Merchant. Each one shook his hand and placed the left hand on his shoulder. "*Sake-t* [friend]" each said. "*Sake-t,*" the Merchant responded. He understood this to be a sign of brotherhood and a covenant of silence. No one would know of their ceremony. Potter embraced the Merchant. "*Kudji sake-t* [Good friend]" he said. "*Kudji sake-t,*" the Merchant repeated. Then:

"What about Big Red and the woman?" he asked.

"Don't worry," Potter said. "They were part of the ceremony."

"They shouldn't get by with this," the Merchant said.

"Don't worry," Potter said again. "They won't."

The Merchant let it go. He wondered how justice could be served by a primeval ceremony. The embers of Andy's cabin glowed red among the pines and against the cold moonscape. Only his iron stove rose stark and phoenixlike above the ashes and embers.

Telling me the story years later, the Merchant was thoughtful. "I left Andy's cabin that night thinking Bessie and Big Red were home free," he said. "The law didn't care a damn about a dead Indian; and anyway, the ceremony was a secret. No one was to talk about it." He looked at me and spread his hands and smiled. "I wondered how a centuries-old, barbaric ceremony would serve justice," he said. "I don't wonder anymore. This is what happened. Believe what you will."

One month exactly to the day of Andy's beating and death, Bessie staggered down Murphys' Main Street. It was late afternoon and growing dark. She was drunk and babbling incoherently. Her face was a mask of blood. Her nose appeared broken and one eye was closed. Her mouth dribbled blood. She held her breasts and moaned. Several men tried to help her. She cursed them. Twice she fell. She screamed Big Red's name. He had beaten her and thrown her out of his shack. It was early February. The temperature hovered between four and nine above. The streets and walkways were slick with ice. Bessie staggered up the hill toward her shack. She disappeared into the dusk. A motorist spotted her body the next morning. She lay near the bottom of a steep, pine-needled hillside. Apparently, she had fallen over the edge of the road, and the ice-glazed and frost-heavy pine needles had shot her down the hillside like a toboggan. She was frozen against the ground. Her body was raised with a loud tearing of cloth and flesh.

The Merchant smiled. "Coincidence?" he said. "Consider what happened to Big Red": Among the Indians a mythology had been building. Happy, he who had pinned the Sheriff's posse down with a burst of gunfire and disappeared into the mountains, had now achieved immortality. He was sighted on a growing number of occasions, moving against the sky on a tall Sierra peak or loping swiftly across a remote valley. A hunter claimed to have met him face-to-face. His eyes were large and expressionless. He said nothing. He disappeared magically before the hunter's eyes. He carried a rifle. He was believed to move between a line of hidden cabins. He was responsible for thefts of food, ammunition, and other items from resort cabins and stores. The thefts were reported from Calaveras to Yosemite. He was believed to have the strength of ten men. He once carried away an iron stove.

A few months after Andy's death, a new myth was begun. A hunter reported seeing a black panther in the Sierra. The hunter was considered reliable enough for the law enforcement agencies of Calaveras and Alpine Counties to check with zoos throughout the state. None reported an escaped black panther. There were other sightings. Wildlife experts laughed at the reports. People were imagining things. They were seeing mountain lions who appeared black against a forested background; the big cats looked dark when in shadows. The experts were puzzled, though, by the numerous reported sightings of mountain lions. The wary beasts were rarely, in fact almost never, seen in the Sierra. Then a middle-aged couple driving down the western slope of Ebbetts Pass, excitedly reported seeing a black panther face-to-face in Hermit Valley, a lush Alpine meadow, high in the Sierra, with a willowed stream flowing through it. It was broad daylight. The creature paused in the middle of the road, lashing its tail and forcing the driver to brake suddenly to a stop. It was coal black. The man said its

eyes were yellow. The woman said they were black. The Indians knew the beast was Whiteman who had, from the eating of
human flesh, metamorphosed into a black panther. In the Indian mind, all things eventually come together in an even
movement; all accounts are settled. And so it was that the leg-
ends and lines of Happy and Whiteman converged among the
towering peaks and in hidden valleys of the Sierra. The two
were glimpsed in the distance, walking together. One man saw
their tracks in the snow at the base of a paleocrystic mountain.
The tracks moved side by side. They paused together and
changed direction. The sightings continued. A man and a black
lion were seen walking together. They were seen through field
glasses by a hunter; they were seen sitting together on a rock.
The man was petting a black lion. They were seen crossing the
Stanislaus River, leaping from rock to rock.

  Some eighteen months after the deaths of Andy and Bessie,
Big Red borrowed a friend's rifle to go deer hunting. The rifle
was a Marlin carbine, caliber .30–.30, serial number L645, Model
93. Big Red was to return the rifle the next day. When three
days passed and Big Red had not returned to Murphys, the
man whose rifle he had borrowed reported him missing, more
from concern for his rifle than for Big Red. On the following
day, Big Red's car was found in Hermit Valley. It was parked
several hundred yards off the road. Hermit Valley is in Alpine
County and thus in the jurisdiction of the Alpine County sheriff, whose office and jail facilities were in Markleeville on the
eastern edge of the Sierra. The sheriff and two deputies brought
bloodhounds to Big Red's car. The dogs took off west, towards
Deer Valley, at full bay. Some five miles into the Mokelumne
River wilderness the dogs bayed treed, but the baying was in-
terspersed with short, impatient barking. That meant the dogs
were puzzled. When the sheriff and his deputies arrived, the
dogs were trotting about a small aspen clearing. They alter-

nately bayed and whined. They kept clustering about a tree against which leaned a rifle, a Marlin carbine, .30-.30, serial number L645, Model 93. The rifle had not been fired. The dogs whined and wagged their tails apologetically. They sniffed the rifle. They would not leave the clearing. There was no sign of a struggle, no indication of foul play. The lawmen took the dogs out several hundred yards to see if they could pick up a scent. The dogs returned to the clearing. For two days, the lawmen scoured the rugged country. On the third day a cold rain turned to snow. The sheriff and his men returned to Markleeville. By morning, the Sierra was locked in snow. Big Red was never seen again.

The Merchant looked at me and smiled. In his smile was a question: "Well?"

"Well," I said. "We know a cat can't turn into a black panther, no matter what it eats."

"Yes," he said, "And we know Big Red couldn't fly, either. Why could the dogs trace him quickly to the clearing where the rifle was found, and then lose the scent? And the rifle. The rifle was placed so it would be the first thing seen when searchers came into the clearing. It was left as a symbol, or a sign."

"What do you think happened?" I asked.

"I don't know what happened," he said. "I know what the Indians believe happened. Happy and Whiteman," he said, "had become immortal. They appeared, visibly, but they left no scent, no tracks. Whiteman carried Big Red off. Happy placed the rifle. They had done this in response to the ritual for Andy. Remember, Potter said that Bessie and Big Red would be taken care of. I was not to worry."

"What about the guy who saw human and cat tracks together on the top of the Sierra?" I asked.

"What about him?" the Merchant asked. "What about all those people who saw the black panther? What about the man and his wife who saw it in front of their car? The people who saw Happy and the cat together?"

I shook my head. I had no response.

"What we know for certain," the Merchant said, "is that Big Red was never seen again."

He laughed. "I want to show you Andy's window," he said. He led me upstairs to his apartment over the store. His living room was spacious. One whole wall was lined with books. There were Indian baskets on shelves and on the floor. Indian blankets were draped over chairs. At the eastern end of the room was Andy's window. There was a large chair in front of it.

"Can you really see Andy's face in it?" I asked.

"Oh yes," he said. "Clearly. He comes with the sun." The Merchant smiled. "You'd see it too, if you had known Andy."

SIX

Dickie

It seems to me now there was never a time when I did not know Dickie and that we have, throughout our lives, been constant companions. It is always with something of a start that I remind myself I have not seen him for thirty years or better. I am not saying he is constantly in my thoughts, nor do I wish to exaggerate our relationship. He simply remains ever green in my mind, the events in our lives are as distinct and vivid as if they had occurred yesterday.

I was six when I first became aware of Dickie. I seem to have always known he was an Indian boy, though I can't recall anyone at home saying anything about him being Indian. Perhaps it was because Dickie's family and mine shared the common bond of poverty and want that did not allow for racial distinctions and which, ironically, might even have enhanced our humanity. And my mother virtually grew up in the center of a rancheria. Nearly all of her father's ranch hands were Indian. Her friends were Indian children.

Dickie and his family lived seventy or eighty yards above us on a flat hilltop at the end of a lane. There were four boys and a girl. In age succession, Jeb was the oldest, followed by Daisy, Billy, Jess and Dickie. The Father arrived in Murphys around 1900. He said he was from Montana. He was half-Irish and half-Sioux. He offered no further information. No one asked. The Father was a big man with black curly hair and a sweeping handlebar mustache, legacies of his Irish father. His mannerisms, though, were Indian. Soft-spoken, he laughed easily and was well-liked. In local parlance "he was not a man to fool with." Early in his life, he had reputedly killed a man in a fair fight. He was respected by both Indian and white. He treated me as if I were his son.

FIG 19. Ramon He Soos's daughter and child.—Rocky Hill, Murphys. Ramon is buried in the Indian "burying grounds" on Rocky Hill. Courtesy Lottie Stephens.

The Mother was a full-blooded Miwok, typically short and stout with a flat-browed and riveled face the color of walnut meats. Her eyes, pressed into an upward slant by high cheekbones, closed when she laughed, which was often. She insisted on instructing me in the Miwok language, beginning where Mary's teaching had ended with her death. She had no guile. Her affection for me was in response to what she felt. I spent as much time with Dickie and his family as I did at home. "You my boy, too, Jackie," she said. "I knew you mama when she little girl." The Father had been a friend of my father, who died while I was a baby. After the custom of his people, he felt a responsibility to me, one that grew into a strong father-son relationship, for which I have been ever grateful. When a white man slapped me for talking back to him, the Father confronted him: "Touch that boy again and I'll kill you," he said and meant it.

Even as a child, I could see that Dickie was his father's son. He bore no resemblance whatever to his three brothers and sister, all of whom were short to average height, stocky, broad-faced with wide, almost flat noses, and thick, spiky hair. Dickie alone reflected the quarter blood of his Siouan ancestry. He was slender and muscular. His legs and arms were long. It was obvious to me even then he would be tall. At fifteen or sixteen, he was over six feet. His nose was thin and aquiline, his face angular and high cheekboned. His shoulder-length hair, though coarse and thick, was lank rather than bristly. Even more distinctive was his bearing. Much later I recalled his essential aloofness, the discernible lineaments of pride in expression, the upward cant of his head, the early touch of arrogance and the quick and deadly flashes of anger. His brothers, though each was different in personality, bore an air of defeat, of subservience. They drank heavily and fought among themselves. They savored the white man's four letter words. Dickie did not walk softly among his older brothers, nor was he intimidated by drunken threats. He seemed to grow taller daily. Ultimately, he reached the height of six-feet-four. From this distance in time, it is possible to see him as a true primitive, the occupant of a time warp who instinctively responded to the call of his blood. In my youthful mind I saw him as a breechclouted, painted, and feathered warrior, a chief astride a pinto stallion. This boyish fantasy does not even today seem exaggerated. The look, carriage, and hauteur of the Plains Indian became more and more pronounced as he grew older. Unlike his brothers who went down to Murphys each evening, Dickie avoided the town. He disliked being around people. On the rare occasion he appeared in town, he was aloof, reserved, dignified. He was never spoken to in the loud jocular manner white men inexplicably reserved for his brothers, and who responded with the obligatory and obsequious self-conscious laugh. He became known as "The Wild Man." He was considered to be sullen, hostile.

To this day, my understanding of Dickie is imperfect. He conceived a friendship and a loyalty to me during our childhood so rare it glows in my mind like light on water. He was an elemental man, a suppliant to both the sun and moon. He was capable of a frightening violence, though it was never even remotely directed to me. His salient mannerism was a roll of his head, which could mean anger or satisfaction. His gesture of friendship was a light tapping on my shoulder with his fist. In time, that shoulder rap became our hallmark. He instinctively grew shoulder-length hair, wore a red headband and a bead necklace. When we were alone, he thrust a hawk feather in his headband. I say instinctively because he could neither read nor write; nor had he ever gone to a movie, thumbed through a picture book or visited an art gallery. Yet he affected the basic accouterments of the Plains Indian warrior. He was anomalous among his people. He rarely acknowledged other Indians (the Father, Mother, and sister Daisy excepted) and when he did it was with an arrogance which, in later years, I found somewhat embarrassing. I recall his periods of silence, of sudden withdrawal when he sat, immobile, gazing into one of our camp fires, his high-boned face glowingly rufescent in the firelight. Was there something in the flames that whispered to him of a past upon which he instinctively acted but never knew? Was his immutable violence, his urge to kill, a response to some sort of primitive turbulence that bubbled up from a Stone Age gene pool? Was he a genetic aberration? The moon held him in thrall. He would stare at it by the hour. He told me he thought of many things; he wondered where the moon came from and where it went. When it became a fingernail he worried that it might not come back. He insisted we dance in celebration, just the two of us, when the moon returned. The moon was sacred. It was not like the sun which held to a steady pattern. Even when it disappeared behind the clouds, the sun gave off the light of day. The moon was independent. It came from time to time, perhaps to look after something the sun had left undone. Dickie considered the moon ineffably female because of "her" whiteness and the softness of her glow. I have often wondered if he ever learned that man had violated the moon by leaving his footprints planted permanently on her, that he had invaded her person and integrity, diminished her with a clutter of debris and abandoned her. I knew that ours was an improbable friendship, and I long ago gave over trying to understand it. No matter. I will always be grateful for it, and some things are best not understood. "He'd kill for you, Jackie," the Father said. "You'll never have another friend like him." He shook his head, "He thinks you will always be together."

One day when I was about sixteen, Dickie and I sat on a log in front of the family house. The Father sat on the porch, quietly talking to Jess. Jeb, the oldest brother, slouched up and stood smirking at us. No one liked Jeb, not even his brothers. Dickie never spoke to him, treated him with contempt. Jeb was regarded locally as a bully and a coward. He was short and squat. His belly bulged over his belt. He was lazy. He caused trouble for the family. The Father watched closely as he continued to talk quietly to Jess.

"Well," Jeb said, "White boy think he's heap big Injun, Injun boy think he's white, gonna be BEEG white man!" He laughed.

I was completely unprepared for what happened. *Shocked*, is a better word.

Dickie simply exploded from the log. I cannot even now

adequately explain that movement. I saw Jeb's insolent smile vanish in a spurt of blood from his nose, heard the thudding blows and Jeb's loud grunt from a fist driven into his stomach that seemed to go all the way to the elbow. There was an explosion of air, a kind of strangled yell, really, and Jeb folded up like a jackknife. Dickie took Jeb's hair in both hands and yanked his head down as he brought up his knee. There was a sickening thump. Jeb fell over, writhing, choking, gasping, spitting blood. I thought he was dying; Dickie had killed him. Almost as if in a dream, I saw Dickie reach down and yank Jeb's head up by the hair and smash him again. He shook a handful of hair from his left hand and grabbed Jeb's hair again.

I heard the Father then. "That's enough," he said. He didn't raise his voice. I had not seen him come up. Dickie still held Jeb's head by the hair, his arm drawn back for another blow.

"That's enough," the Father said again. "Put him down."

I still remember the Father's voice as the sound of soft steel. Dickie dropped Jeb's head and walked off a way and stood with his back to us. Jeb lay gasping and writhing, his face a mask of blood. Jeb never recovered from that beating. "I should've killed him," Dickie said. He did, in effect: Several weeks later Jeb committed suicide, blew his head off with a ten-gauge shotgun. Dickie felt no remorse.

Over the next four years Dickie and I saw each other as often as possible, usually on Sunday afternoons. The Father and Dickie had taken jobs at a sawmill twelve miles north of Murphys. They were housed and boarded by the company and dependent on an occasional ride to and from home. I served my sentence in high school, having earned the distinction of achieving the second lowest grade average in the school's history. Winner of the lowest score was a moron. At least that is the story, gleefully told and retold. I took a job on a ranch where I worked three-hundred-sixty-five days of the year. Work

FIG 20. Indian children—Rocky Hill,
Murphys. Courtesy Bill Harper.

began at 4:00 A.M., often earlier, with a break from twelve to
two. We finished our day around 8:00 P.M. I remained two years
on the ranch, during which time I recall seeing Dickie only a
dozen or so times, and then briefly. When I finally demanded a
day off a month, the rancher fired me.

The year was 1941. War raged in Europe, and the Japanese were
bloodily on the move in the Pacific and in China. The draft
was on, and as much by the scarcity of available young men in
so small a town, I suppose, as by chance, Dickie and I both

received our "greetings" from President Roosevelt. We would be notified when to appear before our local board. Dickie was dismayed. He knew about the almost certainty of the country's involvement in the war; everyone was talking about it, but it simply had never occurred to him that he might be asked to serve. It was not a matter of fear. He was an Indian. It was the white man's fight, not his. He would not go.

Those were confusing days. I don't recall (in fact I'll never really know) who read and explained the draft notice to Dickie and to his family, none of whom could read. Neither do I recall the family receiving mail, though I was later told the Father had, on occasion, asked a friend to read mail for him. The friend must have explained that Dickie could not ignore the summons, that failure to respond would mean his arrest and a jail sentence.

We waited for our "call-up" throughout September. Dickie and the Father got rides to and from Murphys on four consecutive Sundays. On those days, we went to "our pond," a secluded mere deep in the woods and which we considered to be a sacred place. Dickie wore a hawk feather in a red headband. He murmured prayers to the Spirit. We built a fire, smoked a pipe, and blew the smoke in the Four Directions. We made coffee. The pond was filling, and the frogs were in full song. We talked of the first days and nights we had camped here. We talked of running away, going to Nevada, finding an isolated ranch and hiring on. With men going to war, the ranchers would need hands. When the Father heard this, he laughed. He knew we would not go to Nevada. Dickie made his obsequies to the Spirit, and we went home. The Mother and Father hoped Dickie and I would be together if we must go. Ironically, Dickie could have been deferred. Producing lumber was an essential war industry. Years later, The Father told me that he and Dickie had said nothing about the draft to their employer. He did not explain why. When notification came to report to our local draft board in San Andreas on October 8, Dickie informed his employer on the 7th. I can only imagine the reaction. Dickie never mentioned it.

I remember October 8 as an especially beautiful fall morning. The trees lining Main Street had already begun to color yellow and red and deep cyanic patches of sky showed through the foliage, and the street was covered with pools of shade-dappled sunlight that ebbed and flowed to branches waving gently in a light breeze. It was not a day to leave home.

Dickie and I stood in front of the Mitchler Hotel, along with three other "draftees." Dickie's hair hung to his shoulders, and I tried not to think of what would happen when he would be ordered to have it cut. Now he motioned for me to step aside. We walked to a spot overlooking the hotel's Italianate garden. For a moment, he looked out over the bottle-lined pathway, the fishpond, the flowered berms, and carefully placed boulders. His head rolled. He turned to me.

"I'm not going."

"What?"

"Not going."

"Not going. What the hell are you talking about?"

"Not going."

"Well, Jesus …"

"Listen. I only talk Injun."

"Only talk Injun."

"Yes."

"Well hell, everybody knows you talk English."

"The Army don't."

"Well."

"Listen. From now on, we talk only Injun."

"Only Injun."

"In front of people. Savvy?"

"Yes. I guess so."

"Only Injun."

He watched me closely.

"When we get there, you talk for me."

"Talk for you."

"Yes."

"Heap big Injun, you."

"Yes. No talk alla same white man."

"Jesus."

"All right?"

"Yes. All right."

He bumped my shoulder. I was intrigued. Suddenly, it seemed the sensible thing to do, the only thing to do.

"All right," I said again and bumped his shoulder.

A local man had been hired to drive the five of us to San Andreas, where we joined about fifteen other men in front of the Courthouse. Judge J. A. Smith came out and gave us a rousing send off, describing the prodigies we red-blooded American lads would wreak upon the Japs and Germans, should they dare to incur our righteous wrath. Everyone, even the Judge, kept glancing at Dickie. Six-feet-four, now close to two-hundred pounds, black shoulder-length hair, grim of visage, black eyes, aquiline nose and wide mouth that turned down at the corners, Dickie was a spectacular figure. I tried to think of him as a soldier, crew-cut, field cap, necktie tucked into his shirt between the second and third buttons as they appeared in the movies, and all I could see was the red headband and hawk feather. Dickie was right. The Army was not for him.

Now we boarded a bus for Sacramento. Dickie and I sat together near the back. One of the men who sat in front of us turned and asked Dickie how tall he was. Dickie turned to me.

"Six-four," I said. "He doesn't speak English."

"Oh," the man said, and turned around.

Dickie nudged me and nodded slightly. Others had heard us. Word would pass. For emphasis, we tossed a few words back and forth in the Miwok tongue. We had set the scene.

We were taken to the Hotel Clunie in Sacramento and billeted two to a room. At noon, we were given lunch and what was called an "orientation," a harangue, really, by a tough-talking sergeant who urged us to sign up for three years and volunteer for duty in the Philippines where "the women are easy and get whiter every day, *mighty* white." I looked at Dickie. His head was rolling.

"*Keleli! kunatu!*" (White! *shit!*) he muttered.

That evening we were herded across the street to a restaurant for supper. The room was filled, and we sat at long tables. The men stared at Dickie, who, with his wild shoulder-length hair had never appeared more primitive, the dominant figure in a room too small for him, an elemental man conspicuously out of his element. Dickie was tense. I was tense. He knew he was the center of a guarded attention. He held his head too high, his eyes were black, deep wells of ambiguous hostility. I thought all we need is for some loudmouth to trill "whoo, whoo," or say "Hey chief" and World War II will begin right here.

We were marched back across the street by twos. No one was permitted to leave the hotel. Most of the men gathered in the lobby. Dickie and I remained in our room. We were on the second floor. Dickie stood at the window, looking out at the sky.

"Don't worry," I said. "They won't take you."

"I'm not worried about me."

"What, then?"

"You."

"It's only for a year."

"A year. What if there's a war?"

"I'll get you Hitler's mustache."

I walked over to the window. We looked out on cluttered tar paper and composition roof tops and a parking lot. He kept up a nervous tapping of my shoulder.

"I'll go up to our pond and make medicine for you."

"I'll appreciate it."

At ten o'clock someone walked down the hallway, banging on doors and yelling "lights out." We lay on our beds in the dark. Light came in from the window and squared across the floor.

"Jackie?"

"Yes."

"I oughta go with you."

"Worst thing that could happen. You'd kill somebody, and I don't mean Germans and Japs."

"Maybe not."

"First time somebody called you 'chief' or went 'whoo, whoo.'"

"Maybe not."

"When they cut your hair."

He did not answer for some time.

"Maybe they won't."

"No way in hell will they let you keep your hair. You know that. White man heap scalp."

He said nothing. I waited. Finally, I said, "The thing to remember is, you don't speak English. You let me talk for you. All right?"

He didn't answer.

"Dickie?"

In the window light, I saw him nod his head, a glint of tears. I did not press him. I lay awake for a while, then went to sleep.

I awakened to a barely audible sound. Dickie was standing

by the window murmuring his obsequies. I listened for a while, then drifted off. From time to time I awakened, and Dickie still stood by the window. He stood there all night.

At five o'clock in the morning someone banged on our door. "Rise and shine," he sang out. "Drop your cocks and grab your socks." He went from doorway to doorway, and we heard him all down the hallway. I was already up and dressed. Oddly, I kept thinking about the time we camped in a meadow, and Dickie chanted in his sleep. I don't know why I thought of that. Jesus! So long ago.

Dickie was somber, depressed, in a very dangerous mood. I would have to watch him. He wanted desperately to go home. He hated the city, the noise, the men swarming around him. And he was torn, sick with the feeling that he would be deserting me.

"Dickie," I said, "I want you to listen carefully. All right?"

"All right."

"You can't even *think* of going. They'll sure as hell separate us. They'll cut your hair. Someone's bound to call you 'chief' or go 'whoo, whoo.' There's always a loudmouth around. You'd wind up in prison. Understand?"

He nodded *yes*.

"I'd be worried about you all the time."

He nervously bumped my shoulder.

Again I said, "Let me do the talking when the time comes. You *speak no English*. All right?"

"All right."

"Mother and Father need you."

He nodded.

"Daisy too."

Nodded.

"Jess's no help. Neither is Billy."

Again the nod.

There was a bang on the door, a loud voice. "Fall out! Everybody out! Hurry it up! Let's GO!"

Dickie winced, his eyes blinked with each word.

"See what I mean?"

Head lowered, swinging, nodding *yes*.

We went into the hallway and down to the lobby. We were given breakfast in the hotel, another room with long tables. A man moved so Dickie and I could sit together. I thanked him. There was no incident. After breakfast, we were herded out into the lobby. We were not to leave the big room. There was laughter and loud talk. Dickie and I sat on a sofa at the far end of the room.

"Won't be long," I said. "You'll be on your way home."

He said nothing, just looked at me.

"Fall in," someone shouted.

The men began shuffling towards the front door. Dickie and I were the last in line. Outside were three buses, and the men were boarding. We went to the third bus. A man stood by the door counting the men as they climbed aboard. When I stepped on, he put out a hand and stopped Dickie.

"Take the second bus," he said.

Dickie brushed the man aside, violently, nearly knocking him down and climbed on. The man scrambled aboard, yelling "You, you, off the bus!" He came down the aisle.

Dickie turned. I grabbed his arm and pushed by him. The man, it turned out, was the driver. His face was red.

"Out," he said to Dickie, "Out."

"He doesn't speak English," I said. "He's with me."

"I don't give a damn who he's with. Out," he yelled over my shoulder.

"He *has* to be with me. I interpret for him."

"This is my bus, goddam it." He yelled it. "Out."

"All right," I said. I stepped aside. "Put him out."

Dickie was a head too tall for the bus. Hunched over, he looked both enormous and threatening. He started for the driver who backed up, pointing and shouting, "Hold it, hold it," then fled to the front of the bus to the laughter and applause of the men. We found room in the back of the bus, and some of the men patted Dickie as we passed.

"*Kudji nana*," I said. (Good man.) I said it so it would be heard.

The buses started up, and we were driven to a large building. We unloaded and marched by twos inside where we were lined up single file. The line led down a hallway and turned through a wide doorway. I took the position behind Dickie so I could whisper if I had to without him having to turn.

Now I whispered to him: "This is for a physical. Wait until we see what's going on, and I'll tell you what to do."

Dickie's head swung almost constantly. His eyes were big and black. I thought *one wrong move and all hell's going to bust loose.*

We came to the door, and I saw that we had a problem. A mean looking little doctor with a black Hitler mustache, a slit for a mouth, and with absolutely no chin under it, sat on a stool at the head of the line barking shrilly and in a monotone, "Drop your pants, let's have a look. Skin it back and milk it down, bend over, spread your cheeks," as each man came up. His rodent face bore the horrified expression of one who had gazed up a thousand assholes too many, and he kept his head about three quarters averted.

I whispered to Dickie, "*Don't drop your pants, no matter what he says or does.* Just shake your head *no, slowly.* Say nothing. Do nothing. Leave it to me. All right? Understand?"

He nodded. His eyes were black as ink, now, and filled with naked menace.

"Do exactly what I told you. Stand straight, to full height.

Again he nodded and bumped my shoulder.

Dickie came up. The little doctor went through his chant. Nothing happened. He looked up quickly, angrily.

"I said drop your pants."

Dickie shook his head, slowly. Suddenly he was a palpable presence, an unexpected intrusion.

"What the hell's the matter with you? I said drop those *goddam pants.*"

Again, the slow shaking of the head, stretched to full height, looming over the little doctor, eyes black, burning pools.

"That's an order, goddam it," the doctor shrilled, literally bouncing with indignation on his stool.

Everyone was staring. There was an enormous silence. Dickie had glanced at me several times and now the doctor looked at me. I had moved forward.

"You know this man?"

"Yes."

"What the hell's the matter with him?"

"He's an Indian."

"An *Indian!* What the hell's that got to do with it?"

"He won't drop his pants. Indians won't expose themselves. He speaks very little English. A few words."

"Well Jesus H. Christ, if that doesn't take the goddam cake! Every fucking western movie has bare-assed Indians running around, and they *all* speak English.

"This isn't a movie."

The doctor stared up at Dickie.

"Now drop those goddam pants. That's a fucking order, or I'll have 'em taken off."

Dickie's head was beginning to swing. I saw fear in the little doctor's eyes, murder in Dickie's.

"I wouldn't, doctor," I said. "He's nearly killed a man."

Dickie's black eyes never left the doctor's face.

"Well tell him for Chrissake I'm not Custer."

"He's not Custer," I said before I thought. "*Kodja alini Koost-a.*" (House doctor. Not Custer.) The doctor looked at Dickie as if that would bring a relieved response.

"*Kunatu uuten-ko alini Koost-a.*" (Excrement on the doctor and Custer.)

"What'd he say?"

"He said, 'Who is Custer?' He doesn't know anything about Custer. He can't read."

The room was absolutely quiet, not a sound. The men watched, fascinated. The doctor was nervous, sweating. He was becoming a spectacle. He glanced at the waiting line.

"Who sent him here?"

"The draft board."

"Well what the hell for if he doesn't speak English?"

"I don't know."

"I see you talk some Injun."

"Some."

"Tell him he has to, by God, drop those pants."

I stood slightly behind the little doctor who stared up at Dickie.

"*Alini yupte walim, tamma Too-n-o'assen.*" (The doctor wants you to [let down your] rabbit skin robe [so] he [can] kiss your ass.) Dickie never batted an eye, in which there was now a new light. He was home free, and he knew it. Slowly, majestically, he responded.

"*Tcuku alini loc-ta-to-conach-ma kululi.*" (Tell the dog doctor he can kiss my black ass.)

The doctor turned to me. "What did he say?"

"He said he'd rather die. He'll fight. He'll kill someone."

The little doctor jumped up and hurried into another room. Dickie's eye flickered at me.

"*Kudji, kudji,*" (Good, good), I said. You could hear a big wall

clock tick. Some of the men were smiling. The little doctor
with his demeaning and sneering sing-song command was a
man you automatically hated.

In a moment the doctor came back with a big amiable-
looking man whom I later learned was a major. The doctor
was whispering out of the side of his Andy Gump face. The
major nodded, and the doctor returned to his stool. He waved
Dickie and me aside. "Skin it back and milk it down," he shrilled
as the next man stepped up. "Bend over, spread your cheeks."

Now, believe it or not, the major walked over to Dickie,
held up his hand, palm out, and said, "How."

Dickie nodded and solemnly raised his hand for the first
time in his life, with a warning flicker of his eye at me. He was
afraid I'd laugh.

"You no like let doctor have look?" the major said. "See
balls, see cock, see asshole?"

I started to laugh, but again came the warning glance from
Dickie. The major turned to me for translation.

"Well?"

"They don't have those words in their language," I told him.
"No profanity for private parts.

He turned again to Dickie. "You like be heap big warrior?
Fight?"

Dickie looked at me. The major looked at me.

"They don't have warriors," I said. "They didn't have wars.
Not California Indians. They have no word for warrior. Peaceful people."

"You told the doctor this man's violent."

"He can be."

"That he nearly killed a man."

"Yes."

"You said California Indians are peaceful."

"They are."

"What about him?"

"He's half Sioux."

"Half Sioux."

"Yes. Different blood."

"Different from what?"

"Miwok. The other half."

"Miwok. They're not violent."

"No."

"The Sioux part means he's violent."

"Means he can be. Has been."

"Nearly killed a man."

"Yes."

The major stared at Dickie for a moment. Dickie stared back.

"How is it you speak his language but he doesn't speak yours?"

"He refused to learn the white man's language. He knows some words. Not many."

"Refused to learn it. Why?"

"He doesn't like white men."

"Doesn't like white men. What about you?"

"You mean do I like white men or does he like me?"

"Why does he like you?"

"We grew up together."

"Grew up together. And you speak his language."

"Fairly well. Not real good."

The major looked at Dickie. He shook his head. "He'd make one hell of a soldier," he said.

"Yes," I said. "Friends and enemies would all look alike to him."

"I didn't mean that."

He turned to the doctor. "Let him go," he said. He nodded to me. "Take him outside. We'll call a cab. Wait 'til it comes and see that the driver knows where to take him."

He looked at Dickie and raised his hand. Dickie slowly, majestically raised his hand in reply. I thought *this takes the goddam cake.*

As Dickie and I walked out the door, the little doctor was saying, "Skin it back, milk it down, bend over...."

Outside, we punched shoulders. "I didn't know I was half Sioux," Dickie said.

"Just happened. I forgot to tell you." Dickie's eyes were misty. I did not want to see him cry. I kept talking.

"I think the major was suspicious," I said. "That's why he kept asking questions. How'd you like my Injun?"

"Good," he said.

"Heap good?"

"Heap good."

He kept bumping my shoulder. Tears began to well. His head rolled.

"Jackie," he said, and couldn't finish. We did not look at each other. It was a painful moment.

"A year from now, we go to the mountain," I said. "*Muli-ni kome su hisum.*" (Sing to the moon on the mountain.)

The cab pulled up, and Dickie suddenly put both arms around me. He was crying.

"Take care of yourself, Jackie."

"I'll get you Hitler's mustache."

"Take care of yourself." Tears rolled down his cheeks.

"Bus depot," I said to the driver.

When the cab drove off, Dickie looked out the back window and looked until it went out of sight.

I did not see Dickie for sixteen or seventeen years. I am not certain of the length of time. I served four years in the Army, nearly three years in the South Pacific. On my return to the states, I was given the regulation twenty-one day leave, or "de-

lay en route," as it was called, at the end of which I was to
report to a military installation in Santa Barbara, California. I
spent the first three days at home in Murphys. Mother said the
Father and the Mother were living and well. I had almost been
afraid to ask, particularly about
the Mother. Jess, she said, was still
at home and Daisy had married
a "not very bright" white man.
They lived in Mountain Ranch
or West Point. Dickie had had
some trouble, and she did not
know where he was.

"What kind of trouble?"

"I don't know. A fight, I heard.
Several fights."

"Did he go back to work at
the mill?"

"Yes. But I heard they fired
him. I don't know why. The Father stopped by a number of
times to ask about you, but he
did not mention Dickie. I had
the feeling I shouldn't ask."

I went up to the Father's house
in late afternoon of the fourth
day. Coincidentally, it was early
October, three years almost to

FIG 21. Ray Jeff. Full-blood Miwok. World
War II hero. Three Silver Stars, Bronze Star,
five campaign Stars, two Purple Hearts.
Killed on Marshal Island, South Pacific.
Buried on my grandfather's ranch under the
buckeye tree. Courtesy Ray H. Taylor.

the day Dickie and I had left Murphys in response to the draft.
Nothing had changed. It was as if Murphys had existed in a
time warp, waiting. The maples and locusts on Main Street
were red and gold. The big walnut trees in yards were bright
yellow, and the orchard along the lane was a collage of russet
and yellow and red. It had rained recently, and the earth was

dark and smelt of new-settled dust. There were fresh deer tracks in the lane. I had a sense of unreality, of déjà vu. I had imagined this scene so many times and had never expected to see it again. In time, I almost came to believe it existed only in my imagination. The Father's sprawling, tentacled house still hugged the flat behind the live oaks and back of the knoll, a half mile above the house, the walled purlieus of chaparral and manzanita protected the old Indian Burying Grounds and the trail of the ancients, and farther up, the line of hills against the sky were turning blue-grey, and patches of mist had begun to shoal in their hollows.

When I turned in the gate, the Father materialized on the flat's rim as if by some secret understanding. I stopped for a moment and waved. He turned sideways and pretended to fire a rifle, throwing his arms up to its kick. I walked slowly up the hill, savoring the moment, all senses open to the soft hillside earth and the warmth of the sere grass, the smell of the land and of woodsmoke from the house and the big man waiting on the hill. Just below the rim, I paused for a moment. Our first words:

"You get any of 'em Jackie?"

"Did a lot of shootin'"

And then I was on the rim and enveloped in a bear hug. It was a moment when we both groped for words and were embarrassed by our tears, but it was still not an awkward moment.

"Let's go see Mother," the Father said. "She's waiting. You and I'll talk later." Three years had not changed the Father much: a little grayer, wrinkles deeper, no more stooped. We walked slowly toward the house.

"How's Mother?"

"Good. Older, smaller. We all change some."

"Daisy?"

Shook his head. "Married to a white man."

"Jess and Billy?"

"Jess's with Mother. I wanted to meet you alone." He laughed. "Talks more than ever. Billy moved to West Point." Shook his head again. "Billy's gone car crazy, gone white. Works at odd jobs."

"Dickie?" I tried to sound casual, as though I had heard nothing.

"We'll talk later. Let's go see Mother."

When we came to the porch, the Mother rushed to the door.

"Jackie, Jackie," she said softly, crying, "my boy, my *na–a-ti*."

"Mother," I said. "*Uta-ti*. It's been a long time."

"Too long," she said against my shoulder, still crying. I held her. "Too long," she said again. "You come back. I know."

When she finally looked up and smiled the Father said, "Mother it's all right, now." I saw she was older, *tunitci* (smaller), but not three years worth. She seemed browner, her eyes dark in their wrinkled pits, but shining now, almost lustrous.

I felt a bump on my shoulder, and there was Jess. He wrapped both arms around me.

"Jackie, I'm glad the Japs didn't get you."

"Me too," I said, and we all laughed. "*Kuji sake-ti*." (Good friends.) I bumped his shoulder, and he bumped back.

We went into the big living room with its grooved and planked floor. Fascia of venison jerky hung from the hand-hewn oak beams. The long table with its sutured seams like jagged lightening was set with four plates. There was no question as to whether or not I would stay for supper. The Mother held my arm and led me to the table. We sat.

"*Uwu*," The Mother said. "*Ule, yoko, uwuya huku, tuyu tcudjuyu, nupa*." (Eat [There's] bread, deer meat, pinole meal [and] sweet mush.)

The Father kept the conversation on the war, deliberately, I knew.

"Mother had a dream," the Father said. "Then she had a vision. The vision was the same as the dream. She saw you fight. She saw you kill. She saw you come home when the *lika* [tree(s)] color."

"*Hu, Hu, tumku, tumku, yena-ni Tunitci na–a.*" (Yes, yes [you] shoot, shoot [and] kill small man.) The Mother excitedly clapped her hands.

"Japs," The Father said, laughing.

"*Hu, Hu,*" The Mother said.

"You kill any Japs?" Jess asked.

"Like I told Father. I did a lot of shootin'!"

"You kill anything?" he persisted.

"Lotsa trees, bushes, lotsa mountain sides."

"Jess," the Father said.

"*Hock-i-nim,*" the Mother said. "*Uwu.*" (Hungry. Eat.)

Neither the Father, Mother, nor Jess knew I was only on leave and must report for further service in a bit over two weeks. When I told them, the Mother was angry.

"*Ewutu kudji,*" she muttered, "*usutu.*" (No good, bad.)

I assured her I would not have to go back overseas and fight again. I said I would soon be discharged from the Army, that it was almost certain the war would be over soon, and I did not think either Jess or Billy would be called now. We talked of many things that afternoon, of local boys who had been killed or wounded, of how the country might change after the war. There was no discussion of family. Dickie's name was not mentioned.

After the Mother served coffee, the Father turned to me. "Let's talk." As if by prearrangement, the Mother began to clear the table, and Jess and I went outside. Jess asked in a low voice, "Did you kill any Japs?"

"You won't tell?" I said, soto voce.

"No, no," a whisper.

"Promise?"

"Yes, yes, promise."

"You sure?"

"Yes. Sure, sure I'm sure."

I whispered in his ear.

"Between *three and four hundred.*"

He stared at me.

"*Jesus Christ.* How'd you do that?"

"Machine gun. *Mowed* 'em down."

"*Jesus!*"

"Hand grenades. *BOOM!*

He jumped.

"Jesus!"

"Don't tell anyone."

"No. Jesus."

I bumped his shoulder, and he jumped again.

The Father came out. He smiled and shook his head. Jess was still bug-eyed.

"Let's go down back, by the trees," he said. Jess also had been told the Father and I were to have a private talk.

We walked down to the flat and sat under the spreading oak.

"You tell Jess a war story?"

"A whopper."

The Father laughed. "I'm glad they didn't take him. He couldn't have handled it."

"No. Jess'll always be innocent. Good boy."

We sat on the ground and were silent for a while, the kind of silence that readies a man for important talk. The sun was almost down and the earth seemed to glow. A big red-tail hawk, knowing the time for rabbits to come out, sailed down the knoll and landed on the tree top opposite us, teetered for a moment, taking balance with his partly folded wings, settled, and looked at us with deadly accipitral eyes.

The Father began slowly, a few words at a time, long pauses as if he were thinking ahead. Daisy had married a skinny little white man, he said. He tapped his head. "Not very smart. Doesn't work much. Can't hold a job. Ugly little fart, funny pin-head." *I thought Daisy's sure as hell no beauty, but she's intelligent. I felt sorry for Daisy.*

The Father worried about Jess, whether he would ever grow up and take responsibility for himself, what he would do when "Mother and I are gone." He was quiet for some time, looking off to the darkening hills. I had learned early that long pauses in conversation are not embarrassing to Indians as they are to whites, but a time for careful thought, a time to find the right words with which to compose an accurate statement or to offer an important observation. A common Indian plaint holds that the compulsion of white people to speak before thinking is the cause of so many broken promises. In the silence that endured, I felt his need of a question but held back for the present, feeling in my mind for the right time, the proper moment to raise it. He had known me all my life, and he knew I would understand and respect his thoughtful silence.

Only the tips of the hills were visible now, grey welts against the sky; but over the eastern flank of Mt. Davis a luminous glow began, brightened, and in moments a full moon appeared in a dazzling aureole of light that washed over the platinum-grassed hillside. Because of Indian belief in celestial phenomena, I sensed this as the moment, perhaps to the Father, a sign.

"What about Dickie?" I asked, quietly.

The Father leaned forward, picked up a pebble and snapped it away, shook his head, laughed softly.

"He told me how you helped him beat the Army."

"I wish you could've seen us. Did he tell you how the big

major came up and said 'You no like let doctor see balls, see cock, see asshole?'"

The Father laughed his deep, burly laugh.

"Yes. He told me about that. Told me the man came out, raised his hand, and said 'How.'"

"And Dickie raised his. I couldn't believe it. I started to laugh, but Dickie gave me a quick flick of the eye."

The Father leaned back against a tree, rolled and lighted a cigarette, blew out a stream of smoke. Now we would talk.

"When he came home that afternoon," he began, "he was smiling and happy. Mother and Daisy hugged him. He even let Jess punch his shoulder, you know, like you two did. Next day he went with me to the mill, and they hired him right back on. Everybody was glad to see him, gathered round, shook his hand."

Again, a long and thoughtful silence. Inexplicably, I suddenly *thought of New Guinea and the jungle dripping rain, the cloud-circled peaks where the Japs were dug in, the seashore and the pounding waves at night, the Southern Cross, the big muddy rivers that seemed to slide rather than flow and the little soldier caught by a crocodile and the banzai attacks; and why in hell did I think all the time of the place where I'm sitting now when I was in New Guinea; and now here, I think of New Guinea.*

I waited.

"He was happy, maybe three, four days, then changed. First got quiet, head began that roll, you know, swinging back and forth, stayed to himself." There was another pause. I knew my presence gave him the chance to think aloud, to put his thoughts and fears into words, the better to understand them, to see them.

"One day Jess bumped his shoulder, been doing it, and Dickie jerked him off his feet, and if I hadn't spoke quickly, might've been like Jeb all over again."

He sort of smiled in the bright moonlight, shook his head. It was the first time I had heard Jeb's name mentioned since his death. More than anything, that told me how serious the Father was.

"Got into a fight over nothing at the mill. Then another. Foreman warned him: one more fight and he was out." Again, shook his head. "Two days later he had another fight. Took half a dozen men to stop him. Fired him on the spot." Long silence, brushing his hand back and forth across the grass. I sensed that this was not the time to speak.

"He had moved into one of the rooms that opened on the main part of the house. The night of the day he'd been fired, I heard him get up and leave the house. I got up and watched him. He walked down the hill. I hadn't seen a gun, but thought he might have a pistol. I ran down the hill." The Father looked off to the hills, picked up a stick and stirred at the grass.

"Didn't have a gun. I asked him what he was doing. Said he wasn't 'afraid of going to war.' He should've gone. He could've helped you. If you 'got killed or hurt, it was his fault.'"

"I said Jackie knew the Army wasn't for you. He was right. Wasn't your fight anyway. He said, 'I'm not talkin' about the goddam Army. I'm talkin' about Jackie.'

I waited.

"I got him to come up to the house and go to bed. Two days later he left. Went to West Point."

There was another long pause. He looked at me, his face illuminated in the bright moonlight.

"What then?"

"Worked here and there." Another long silence.

"Started to drink."

"Where is he now?"

Again the slow shaking head.

"Don't know. West Point, Mt. Ranch, Sonora, Jimtown, Standard." Shrugged.

"He's lived in all those places?"

"All of 'em. Others."

"How long since you've seen him?"

"Two months, three. More, I guess. More."

"I wish I could look for him," I said. "Problem is gasoline. You know it's rationed."

"I know."

"I was given just enough tickets or coupons for gas to report to Santa Barbara."

He nodded. We sat quietly for a time, looking out across the moon-ripe hills. After a while I said, "The war should be over soon. I'll be discharged and gas rationing will be ended. We'll look for him. We can go to the mountain."

The moon was high, now, and up over the knoll and the Burying Grounds coyotes began to sing. "Never thought I'd ever hear a coyote again."

He laughed. "I saved 'em for you."

We walked up to the rim and looked across town. I had difficulty taking my leave. I sensed there was something else to be said. I told him I would ask around to see if anyone had seen Dickie. He nodded and looked across the town, then lowered his head.

"There's something else," I said.

He sighed, waggled his head, gave a short, mirthless laugh. "He has a white woman now."

In the next four or five days, I asked a lot of questions around town, and I heard a lot of stories, to which there was a general consistency. Dickie was quarrelsome, violent, had a lot of fights, drank, in fact was drunk much of the time, couldn't hold a job, was undependable, moved about constantly. The story of Dickie's white woman was related with gleeful and repugnant salacity. Like Daisy's husband, she apparently was not very bright. She was promiscuous but her promiscuity was of the dull, nonprurient manner of the working prostitute. Dickie was wildly jealous. A more volatile combination I could not imagine. No one knew where he, or they, were living at the moment. These things I told the Father on my last visit before reporting to Santa Barbara. The only thing he did not already know was the general character of Dickie's white woman. He was not surprised. He shrugged. "What else?" he said.

Supper that night was a sad affair. The Mother was subdued. Even Jess seemed at a loss for words. The Father and I tried to keep a conversation going, but there were long moments of silence. When I left and embraced the Mother, she cried almost convulsively. Jess kept tapping my shoulder. I had assured her throughout the evening I would comeback, that the war would soon be over. The Father gently disengaged her. "Jackie'll be back, Mother," he said. "He'll be back."

We walked to the flat's rim. I kept my moments of a respectful and thoughtful silence with difficulty. We looked out across the town, to the old school house, to the caesura of red sky that was Johnson's Gap, to the muted lights of Murphys. (I had to smile to myself when I thought of Murphys observing a blackout during the war.) In the distance, there was the haunting and detached bawl of a cow, a disembodied note that drifted and floated so it was hard to fix bawl to body, to a sure-enough cow standing four-legged and bawling for a calf or just into the open night. It seemed an omen of some sort. I felt depressed. It was the Father who spoke first.

"Mother dreamed you won't be coming back," he said, "not for a long time. Maybe never."

I shook my head. "I don't think dreams mean anything. Two nights ago I dreamed I was back in New Guinea. I'll never be sent back there. I've also dreamed I could fly."

He laughed.

"Do you believe in dreams?" I asked.

He shook his head. "No. Mother does and so do the kids."

It was an awkward leave taking, for both of us. We had trouble talking. He suddenly embraced me.

"Come back," he said.

"I will."

He turned quickly and walked toward the house. I walked down the familiar old hill, tears running down my face.

Because of hearing loss from shell explosions and prolonged heavy machine gun firing next to my ear, I was transferred from the infantry and assigned to Special Services in Santa Barbara. I was discharged in mid-September of 1945. I had learned that every veteran, regardless of his or her high school record, was entitled to enroll in the college or university of choice under the G.I. Bill of Rights. The student would be on probation for a year. Failure to maintain at least a C average for the first year meant dismissal. A successful first year entitled the "candidate" to a full four years. I enrolled at the University of California, Santa Barbara College, and graduated in 1949. I worked six months, then moved to Palo Alto, California, where I began graduate work at Stanford University. In 1955, I took a position as American History instructor at San Jose City College. Later, I introduced American Indian History into the curriculum and taught it.

During the sixteen or seventeen year period when I did not see Dickie, I experienced the gamut of emotions, from guilt to frustration. I knew that ours was an irreconcilable relationship, had known it even before the war. There was no logical or possible way to continue it. Yet we had forged a friendship so compelling he had nearly killed for me. He was an Indian who was unable to be Indian, and most certainly not a white man's Indian. He had reached a dead end while for me life was just beginning.

I did not mean to imply that I have passed these years ago- nizing over a relationship that was, from its inception, destined to an abrupt end. My future lay open to whatever talents I might possess and to wherever my ambitions would take me. His was ordained by race and culture, and by bigotry. Events in our lives have remained profoundly clear and ever current in my mind while other significant ones, such as the war itself and the collegial refutation of my high school record have faded, become unimportant. Dickie was, I knew, a highly intelligent and complex individual. His wonder at the moon and other celestial phenomena might have, could have, in a different sys- tem than ours (where the frontier mentality still obtains), been directed to a study of astronomy. I recall the wistful note in his words the night I explained the moon's cycles: "I wish I could read."

I had long nursed a sense of obligation to Dickie and to the Father and Mother, one kept green by the study and teaching of Indian History and for which profession they were the in- spiration. I took great satisfaction, of course, in teaching about them (and about Miwok people), but I wanted to write or record their personal story as I knew it and for nearly eighteen years was privileged to be a part of it. And while the Father and the Mother were integral to the family saga, as were other fam- ily members to a lesser extent, the story is really about Dickie.

Over the years, I searched for Dickie, though there were protracted intervals between searches. (It was during these searches that I learned the Father and Mother had died. It was several years before I learned of the Mother's passing. There was very little note taken of an Indian's death.) Nevertheless, I managed to cover the counties of Amador, Calaveras and

Tuolumne, and a dozen or more towns. Always Dickie seemed to have just moved on, leaving behind him a growing reputation for violence.

Then one day on a weekend visit with my mother in Murphys, I was about to cross the street by the Corner Store. I did not look at the car approaching the intersection from the east, that is, from behind me, but paused to let it pass. When it swung around directly in front of me someone yelled, "STOP!" and the car slammed to a halt. I still had not focused on the people in the car. Then I heard "JACKIE!"

Dickie was seated between two young Indian women in the back. A young girl, also Indian, drove. Now he had the door open and was crawling out, head first, right over the lap of the woman on my side of the car. He braced himself by his hands on the ground and struggled to his feet by hanging on to the car. He was dead drunk. He staggered towards me, his arms outstretched.

"Jackie," he yelled. "By God."

"Dickie. I've looked all over hell and gone for you." The only emotion I recall (if it can be called an emotion) is surprise.

His eyes were half-closed. He was slack-jawed and his teeth, which I remembered as white and strong, were rotted black snags. Spittle drooled down his chin. His hair was cut short. He threw his arms around me. He smelled. There was dried vomit on his shirt.

"Jackie. By God."

"Dickie. It's been too damn long."

"What's too damn long?"

"Since I saw you."

"Since I saw you," he repeated.

Then, "Jackie. By God. Jackie. My wife's dead. Dead an' gone to heaven."

"I'm sorry, Dickie. What happened?"

"Jackie. Dead and gone to heaven."

"What happened?"

"What happened. Deadern' a doornail."

"What happened?"

"What happened. Put my .30–06 in her mouth. BOOM! BOOM! Blowed her fuckin' head clean off. Clean to the ceiling. BOOM! Blowed her to heaven."

He threw up his arms at each "boom," and I could imagine the explosion of her head, flying chunks of skull, brains, and hair smashed against the ceiling, blood dripping.

"My God!"

"My God," he repeated. Then he raised his arms and aimed an imaginary rifle and yelled "POW!"

"You didn't get me Hitler's mustache."

I was speechless for a moment, mentally suspended somewhere between a blown-off head and Hitler's mustache.

"Hitler's mustache," he said again. "You didn't get it."

"No," I said. "No I didn't.

"He shave it off?"

"No. No, I went to the Pacific."

"He shaved it."

"Yes. Shaved it. I went to the Pacific."

All these years I've looked for him and we talk goddam crazy nonsense.

"To the P'cific. Where the fuck's that?"

"Out in the ocean."

"In the ocean."

"Pacific ocean."

He looked mean. He stared. I thought it best to keep him talking.

"I tried to get Tojo's balls for you but he didn't have any."

"Tojo's balls."

"Tojo's balls. Yes."

"No balls. You didn't get 'em."

"No. No balls."

"Who's Tojo?"

"Big Jap."

"Big Jap."

"No balls."

"No balls."

Nearly twenty years for this. This is it.

I pointed to the girls in the car.

"All those girls your daughters?"

He looked towards the car, then turned to me.

"Where? What girls?"

"In the car."

"In the car."

"Yes. Are they your daughters?"

"In the car." He threw his head back and pounded his chest. "That's my *WUKITAH*! [cunt]" He almost yelled it.

I saw the girls understood. They all turned and looked out the opposite side of the car. One kept shaking her head. I couldn't think of anything to say. I was embarrassed for them. He stood swaying and shuffling his feet to keep his balance, drooling. He turned suddenly and started for the car. Then he came back.

"Jackie. Come see me."

"I will."

"You will."

"Yes. Where do you live?"

"Where do you live."

"Where do *you* live?"

"Where do I live."

"Yes."

"I live … Sheep Ranch. Sheep Ranch."

"Sheep Ranch. I'll come see you."

"See me."

He started for the car again, and again turned back. He looked closely at me for a moment, bending down and weaving side to side, then slowly reached out and bumped my shoulder. I bumped him back, and he turned, stumbled, and crawled into the car between the two young women. He stared at me as they drove off.

Our first meeting after all those years lasted about twenty incoherent minutes, probably less. I could only think of it as bitterly disappointing and above all, tragic. I had expected at least some semblance of the old Dickie. I had not, apparently, listened closely to the stories about him or, as a psychologist friend suggested, I subconsciously rejected them. It is my personal belief the powerful image of the towering, long-haired, head-banded warrior with the occasional hawk feather was so firmly impressed upon my mind or imagination, I couldn't conceive of the shambling drunk and uncharacteristically loud wreck of a man who suddenly and unexpectedly crawled head first out of a car yelling my name. His only indication or recognition of our years together was the bump on the shoulder and, incongruously, the inane babbling about Hitler's mustache. What seemed especially tragic, grotesque would perhaps be a better word, was his loud, obscene, gesticulatory (and mercifully brief) account of his wife's suicide and almost in the same breath, "Pow! You didn't get me Hitler's mustache."

Midway through our meeting, I had wanted only to get it over with, to end it, to stop babbling gibberish. I had had no intention of visiting him in Sheep Ranch. To his "come see me," I said I would so as not to delay his departure or perhaps create a problem. That last minute bump on the shoulder, though, whether reflexive or an afterthought, evoked a warm flood of old feelings and images. The warrior vision I had lived with for so long was too powerful, too deeply etched in memory and experience to be effaced or even much diminished, by a fifteen to twenty minute chance meeting with a sodden caricature. That bump reverberated across the years. I would go to Sheep Ranch.

As I prepared to leave Murphys Sunday morning for San Jose via Sheep Ranch, my mother said, "I don't know why you're doing this. What do you expect to find?"

"I don't know, Mom. Maybe he'll be sober. Maybe I can help him."

"Help him? How?"

"I don't know."

"Are you doing it for him, or for yourself?"

"For both of us, I guess."

"I never heard of his wife's suicide."

"Well, it was the first thing he blurted out, and in bloody detail."

"It would've been in the papers."

"Maybe not. An Indian and a white woman. You know."

"All the more reason they'd publish it."

"Mom, I feel that I have to make the effort. I owe him that."

"You said his teeth are black and rotten. They didn't get that way over night."

"I know."

"Well, I just don't want you to be disappointed."

"I know what to expect now."

Actually, I had no idea of what to expect. As I drove to Sheep Ranch, I tried to imagine what I would find: Dickie sober and regretful of our first meeting after all those years; Dickie drunk again; shacked-up with the three young girls; belligerent, perhaps downright hostile. Penitent. Whatever.

The small scatter of Indian shacks had arrogated to themselves a gently sloping pine-needled hillside on the northeast entrance to town, each one vermiculate and silvered with tracery and sagging towards the earth waiting to receive them, tiny fragile islands in a wilderness of abandoned and patinated auto carcasses and scattered parts, old wagon bodies, broken wheels, and utensils. There was only one car parked between two shacks that looked as if it might run, but it was not the one that Dickie had shared with the three girls. I saw only a single person, an elderly, white-haired man who, when I slowed down, hurried into his shack. I decided to by pass the Indians, none of whom I knew and talk to the Merchant, who was respected and liked by the Indians and whom I had known since childhood.

The Merchant's store was closed Sunday, but he welcomed me with open arms, literally. Robust and zestful at eighty or better, he laughed and said, "I know your visit has something to do with Indians, but first, fresh-brewed coffee. Sit down."

He poured coffee into large blue mugs and pulled up a chair. It was like the old times when he told me Andy's story. He held his mug as if it were a ciborium.

"Well," he said. "Dickie?"

I laughed. "Dickie. Yes."

I told him of my meeting with Dickie and of his story of his wife's suicide, during which time he nodded as though he had heard it all before.

"He asked me to come see him. He said he lived in Sheep Ranch."

"Yes," he said. "I thought that was it. Well, he hasn't lived in Sheep Ranch for three years or better. Better."

"I never knew him to lie."

"He's not lying. His mind is gone. He destroyed it with booze."

"He remembered me. He remembered Hitler's mustache. He bumped my arm." I then explained the arm-bumping.

"He told you he lived in Sheep Ranch, too. That graphic

description of his wife's or woman's suicide is pure fantasy. She left him. She lives near Avery. Let me tell you Dickie's story as I learned it from Indian friends: Dickie built his life around you. In his mind it would always be the two of you. He never imagined another kind of life. He did not try to make new friends. He could not conceive of you both eventually going different ways. The war changed your lives abruptly. You were gone, gone for years. Had your separation taken place over a longer period of time, well, who knows?"

He paused for a moment. "Bother you to hear this?"

"Yes. I want to know."

"Well, Dickie felt he'd abandoned you. He was sure you'd be killed. It would be his fault. He should have gone with you. He was drunk for days on end. He had the snakes. He was arrested for shooting monkeys off fence posts. The monkeys were throwing rocks at his shack."

"Jesus. I feel I let him down somehow."

"How? By not giving up your life to play Indian?"

"It wasn't play with Dickie."

"You had a rare friendship, as rare as they get. I had one, too, as you know, with Andy. You damn well learned in the war that nothing's forever. We are both privileged to have known them for awhile."

"I was wondering. Could he be so far gone, so completely addled he sees or imagines Jeb's suicide as his wife's? She 'blowed her fuckin' head clean off' by putting my .30–06 in her mouth' just as Jeb did?" I held up my fingers to symbolize quotes.

"Well, yes. Anything's possible, I guess. But why worry it like you're doing? What's the point?"

"None, probably."

"Forget it. Remember the good days."

"I was just thinking out loud."

We shook hands.

"Don't be so scarce," he said.

"I won't."

As I drove home, I thought of the towering warrior with the red headband and the necklace and hawk feather.

I saw Dickie for the last time nearly five years later, and again it was in Murphys. Between eight and nine o'clock of a summer evening gravid with tarweed-scented breezes and the rich, loamy earth-smell of water flowing bankfull in open irrigation ditches, mother and I were talking about my late afternoon sojourn in the Murphys Cemetery, wandering among the menhirs of the "departed" in an unsuccessful effort to locate the graves of the Father and Mother.

"I can't find a trace of them."

"Well," mother said, "how long's it been, twenty-five years?"

"About."

"Well."

"I think they buried people right on top of them."

"I wouldn't be surprised."

"Nothing's marked."

I was thinking of the skeletal immurement and commingling of Indian and white on the pine-needled hillside, ironically equal at last in the purlieus of the deceased, when someone came onto the outer porch and rapped on the door. It was a friend whom I had known from childhood. There was a quick, urgent handshake, no amenities. He was much agitated. He wished to speak to me in private. Outside another old friend stood at the bottom of the steps, his hand resting on the newel post. He nodded.

"Jack," he said.

"What is it, what's going on?"

"Your friend," he said. "Dickie."

"*Dickie?* What about him?"

"He's got the hotel bar hoorawed. Got a big hunting knife and won't let anyone leave. He's standing on the bar and ..."

"*On* the bar?"

"Hell yes! flapping his arms and crowing like a goddam rooster and making noises like a train whistle. He runs up and down on the bar and points that big goddam knife when anyone tries to leave."

"You call the sheriff?"

"Yes, but the sheriff and his deputies are out somewhere."

"What the hell am I supposed to do?"

"You know him. He's your friend."

"Oh. I just go down and in the name of old friendship take his 'big goddam knife' away."

"Maybe you can talk to him. You know."

"Look. I've seen him *once* in twenty-five years. *Once*. For *fifteen minutes*. He was gone, drunk, wiped out. Said he lived in Sheep Ranch. He hadn't lived there for three years. Said his ..."

"Does now."

"Does what?"

"Lives in Sheep Ranch."

"Well."

"Listen, Jack, if you could just come down, see for yourself. Maybe if he sees you."

"Maybe what?"

"Well."

"Were you two in the bar?"

"Yes."

"How did you get out?"

"We were at the lower end of the bar, by the hall door, when he jumped up on the bar and began crowing and tooting and waving that knife. We slipped through the door and ran out the back."

"Maybe he's down now."

"No. We went around front and looked through the glass doors. He's up there, flapping and tooting."

"Where did he hear a train whistle?"

"Stockton. Someone took him to Stockton. He heard a train. Now he wails like one whenever he's drunk."

Mother came to the door. The men nodded to her.

"What happened?"

"Nothing. Dickie's at the hotel, drunk. They want me to talk to him."

"Well, it's not your problem."

"Won't hurt to talk to him."

"Won't do any good, either."

"Well, I'll try."

We drove to the hotel and parked around the side, back of a stand of locust trees where Dickie told me he was not going into the Army. We heard Dickie before we got to the door. "Er er erc erc errr rrroo."

"Rooster."

"Yes."

"Waaaow, waaaow. Whoo, whoo."

"Train."

"I hear."

We looked through the glassed doors. Dickie stood on the bar holding out a long-bladed hunting knife which flashed ominously when it caught the light. He looked enormous up on the bar, frightening. No wonder no one moved. His hair was a little longer, his mouth gaping, eyes half-closed. He threw his head back and flapped his arms.

"Er, er erc erc rrrroooo."

He looked around the room, pointing and thrusting with the knife, as if he expected applause. Then he cupped both hands around his mouth, holding the knife between his thumb and forefinger.

"Waaaaaoww, waaaow."

"What do you think?" Tom asked.

"He's pretty good."

"I don't mean that."

"I don't know. That's a wicked knife." *What if the deputies come and shoot him. He fought for you.*

We watched him crow and wail like a train. It was weird, frightening, primal. He walked up and down on the bar. He slashed the air with the knife. He did not speak. *This was the man I camped with.*

"All right," I said. "I'm going to open the door and step inside and try to talk to him. But *keep the door open.* Don't let it close. If he jumps off the bar with that knife, we run."

"All right."

I opened the door slowly. Everyone whirled to look. Dickie crouched and pointed his knife at me. *He'd kill for you Jackie The Father said you'll never have another friend like him he'd kill for you, kill …*

"Hello, Dickie."

He stared, crouching. There was no recognition in his eyes. He jabbed the knife towards me.

"It's Jackie."

I stepped a little closer.

"Jackie," I said again.

He straightened and started to crow. He flapped his arms. "Er er erc …" He never took his eyes off me. He started again and stopped.

"Jackie. Your friend."

I moved closer. There was a dead silence. You could hear people breathing. I thought of the soldier who said *I was so scared you could hear me sweat.*

He tried again. "Er erc …" and trailed off.

"Dickie?"

FIG 22. Buckeye tree. Large Indian burial site.(Ray Jeff's stone in foreground)— Saunders Ranch. Photo by author.

"Waa wh …" a half-hearted flap of his arms. He threw up his arms again, held them for a moment, then let them drop.

I sensed the moment. I walked to the bar and looked up at him.

"Dickie, its *Jackie*."

He stood up straight, never taking his eyes off me.

"The knife, Dickie. Give me the knife." I held out my hand. "*Kitce*."

We locked eyes. There was no recognition in his. He said nothing.

"Dickie? The knife. *Kitce, kitce*."

Slowly he turned the knife and handed it down to me, haft first. I passed the knife to someone behind me and reached up to Dickie.

"Come on down. *Walim, tamma.*" I put up my hand. "*Walim, tamma.*" (Get down.).

He took my hand and stepped down. Outside a red light flashed. I told the men who had come to the house to hold the deputies back. Dickie paid no attention to the red light or to the sheriff's car. He kept staring at me. The two young deputies stood, waiting. There were no drawn guns. The oldest one turned off the red light and came forward. Dickie stood behind me.

"What do you want us to do?" he asked.

"Will you take him home, to Sheep Ranch?"

"He was flashing a knife."

"He never threatened anyone. He was doing his rooster and train act."

"His what?"

"Rooster and train act. Crowing like a rooster and wailing like a train."

"Where's the knife?"

"I took it. Handed it to someone."

"He just gave it up?"

"Yes."

The two deputies stared at Dickie.

"Big man."

"Yes. My closest friend."

"Friend."

"Yes."

Dickie stood quietly behind me.

"We'll take him home," the deputy said. He looked at his partner who nodded.

I thanked him and opened the back seat door of the patrol car. Dickie climbed in and sat looking at me through the window. Just as the car started, he opened the door and got out.

The deputies started to scramble. I held up my hand. Dickie stood for a moment, looking steadily at me, then slowly reached out and bumped my shoulder. I bumped him back. "*Kudji sake-t,*" I said, "*kudji sake-t*" (Good friend, good friend). He turned and got back into the car. He watched me through the window until the car turned and went out the Sheep Ranch road.

Afterword

After California's centennial year, in 1949, there was a kind of Indian renaissance, now that they were gone. Every Old-Timer had his or her sentimental story to tell, a pet bit of nostalgia. The Indians had been "true blue" and "loyal friends." They were also noble and prophetic, possessed of scientific secrets of longevity, were a great and imaginative people. The writing is even worse. A local and unquestionably kindly woman, a Murphy's Old-Timer who knew many of the old Indians concluded a two-page essay entitled "Indians" with these words: "The *rancheria* is deserted now. . . . No more pow-wows. . . . Their little huts long have been obliterated . . . the noble Round House is gone. All the relics of their happy, carefree days are gone, gone forever. Hail and farewell, friends of our childhood."

Much of what is written is equally lachrymose, maudlin, and unreal. If one can associate "happy" and "carefree" days with a period that witnessed mutilation, murder, discrimination of the cruelest sort, the reduction of a people to beggary

FIG 23. Mortar rock. Saunders Ranch. Called
"Coconut Rock" because holes resemble
marks on coconuts. Photo by author.

and finally, to near-extinction, one possesses the remarkable
capacity to insulate oneself against history.

Well, its "hail and farewell," all right. To see an elderly Miwok
today is as rare as to observe the flight of a trumpeter swan.
They are gone, vanished, leaving only impressions on the land
to mark their passage. Over there, under that Digger pine is a
quartz outcropping pocked with mortar holes; below Walker's
cabin, under a ledge, are the holes where his *mahala* (woman)
ground acorns. At the edge of a field, by heavily traveled road-
sides, in flats along stream banks are the mortared rocks, all that
is left of a culture, pounded into stone. Sacred burial grounds
are disappearing under sprawling subdivisions.

On a recent spring morning after a cool rain, I walked up
the knoll on my grandfather's ranch, now a deep lupined blue,
past the wide shade of the buckeye tree and the burying ground
where Reed and his mother, now long forgotten, are buried,
to the big mortar rock. It was filled with clear water. And I
could see, reflected back, an old and wrinkled Indian face.